INTRODUCING
ISSUES WITH
OPPOSING
VIEWPOINTS®

Homelessness

Noël Merino, *Book Editor*

GREENHAVEN PRESS
A part of Gale, Cengage Learning

GALE
CENGAGE Learning·

Detroit • New York • San Francisco • New Haven, Conn • Waterville, Maine • London

Elizabeth Des Chenes, *Director, Publishing Solutions*

For more information, contact:
Greenhaven Press
27500 Drake Rd.
Farmington Hills, MI 48331-3535
Or you can visit our Internet site at gale.cengage.com

Articles in Greenhaven Press anthologies are often edited for length to meet page requirements. In addition, original titles of these works are changed to clearly present the main thesis and to explicitly indicate the author's opinion. Every effort is made to ensure that Greenhaven Press accurately reflects the original intent of the authors. Every effort has been made to trace the owners of copyrighted material.

Cover image © Con Tanasiuk/Design Pics/Corbis.

LIBRARY OF CONGRESS CATALOGING-IN-PUBLICATION DATA

Homelessness / Noël Merino, book editor.
    pages cm. -- (Introducing issues with opposing viewpoints)
  Includes bibliographical references and index.
  ISBN 978-0-7377-3851-3 (hardcover)
  1. Homelessness--Juvenile literature. 2. Homelessness--United States--Juvenile literature. I. Merino, Noël.
  HV4493.H657 2013
  362.5'92--dc23
                                                                  2012049718

Printed in the United States of America
1 2 3 4 5 6 7 17 16 15 14 13

Contents

Chapter 3: How Should Legislation Address Homelessness?

Foreword

I ndulging in a wide spectrum of ideas, beliefs, and perspectives is a critical cornerstone of democracy. After all, it is often debates over differences of opinion, such as whether to legalize abortion, how to treat prisoners, or when to enact the death penalty, that shape our society and drive it forward. Such diversity of thought is frequently regarded as the hallmark of a healthy and civilized culture. As the Reverend Clifford Schutjer of the First Congregational Church in Mansfield, Ohio, declared in a 2001 sermon, "Surrounding oneself with only like-minded people, restricting what we listen to or read only to what we find agreeable is irresponsible. Refusing to entertain doubts once we make up our minds is a subtle but deadly form of arrogance." With this advice in mind, Introducing Issues with Opposing Viewpoints books aim to open readers' minds to the critically divergent views that comprise our world's most important debates.

Introducing Issues with Opposing Viewpoints simplifies for students the enormous and often overwhelming mass of material now available via print and electronic media. Collected in every volume is an array of opinions that captures the essence of a particular controversy or topic. Introducing Issues with Opposing Viewpoints books embody the spirit of nineteenth-century journalist Charles A. Dana's axiom: "Fight for your opinions, but do not believe that they contain the whole truth, or the only truth." Absorbing such contrasting opinions teaches students to analyze the strength of an argument and compare it to its opposition. From this process readers can inform and strengthen their own opinions, or be exposed to new information that will change their minds. Introducing Issues with Opposing Viewpoints is a mosaic of different voices. The authors are statesmen, pundits, academics, journalists, corporations, and ordinary people who have felt compelled to share their experiences and ideas in a public forum. Their words have been collected from newspapers, journals, books, speeches, interviews, and the Internet, the fastest growing body of opinionated material in the world.

Introducing Issues with Opposing Viewpoints shares many of the well-known features of its critically acclaimed parent series, Opposing Viewpoints. The articles are presented in a pro/con format, allowing readers to absorb divergent perspectives side by side. Active reading questions preface each viewpoint, requiring the student to approach the material thoughtfully and carefully. Useful charts, graphs, and cartoons supplement each article. A thorough introduction provides readers with crucial background on an issue. An annotated bibliography points the reader toward articles, books, and websites that contain additional information on the topic. An appendix of organizations to contact contains a wide variety of charities, nonprofit organizations, political groups, and private enterprises that each hold a position on the issue at hand. Finally, a comprehensive index allows readers to locate content quickly and efficiently.

Introducing Issues with Opposing Viewpoints is also significantly different from Opposing Viewpoints. As the series title implies, its presentation will help introduce students to the concept of opposing viewpoints and learn to use this material to aid in critical writing and debate. The series' four-color, accessible format makes the books attractive and inviting to readers of all levels. In addition, each viewpoint has been carefully edited to maximize a reader's understanding of the content. Short but thorough viewpoints capture the essence of an argument. A substantial, thought-provoking essay question placed at the end of each viewpoint asks the student to further investigate the issues raised in the viewpoint, compare and contrast two authors' arguments, or consider how one might go about forming an opinion on the topic at hand. Each viewpoint contains sidebars that include at-a-glance information and handy statistics. A Facts About section located in the back of the book further supplies students with relevant facts and figures.

Following in the tradition of the Opposing Viewpoints series, Greenhaven Press continues to provide readers with invaluable exposure to the controversial issues that shape our world. As John Stuart Mill once wrote: "The only way in which a human being can make some approach to knowing the whole of a subject is by hearing what can be said about it by persons of every variety of opinion and studying all modes in which it can be looked at by every character of mind. No wise man ever acquired his wisdom in any mode but this." It is to this principle that Introducing Issues with Opposing Viewpoints books are dedicated.

Introduction

"We pay a steep price for homelessness as a nation."

—Kathleen Sebelius, secretary of the US Department
of Health and Human Services, July 17, 2012

Homelessness in America is a problem nationwide. It takes a heavy toll on families, communities, and individuals. One of the ways in which homelessness takes a toll is by exacting a financial cost. Homelessness costs communities and taxpayers thousands of dollars through emergency shelters, hospitalization and medical care, police intervention, incarceration, and other services. There is widespread debate about the best way to address homelessness in a cost-effective manner, but what is beyond dispute is that homelessness is a costly social problem.

According to a 2010 study by the US Department of Housing and Urban Development (HUD), "The emergency shelter system may be an 'adequate' response to an immediate housing crisis for most individuals, but is an expensive solution to family homelessness."[1] According to HUD, average homeless system costs for first-time homelessness for individuals ranged from $1,634 to $2,308, whereas for families it ranged from $3,184 to $20,031. The study found that the cost of providing emergency shelter is not always the least expensive housing option. For individuals, overnight emergency shelters are less expensive than transitional or permanent supportive housing but generally offer fewer services. However, for certain populations, permanent housing proves to be vastly less expensive: A program in Seattle, Washington, that provided permanent housing for chronically homeless individuals with severe alcohol problems found that its costs per person per month fell after six to twelve months in permanent housing from $4,066 to $1,492. The HUD study did find that, for families, transitional or permanent supportive housing was no more expensive—and often less expensive—than emergency shelters.

Partly because the majority of homeless people lack health insurance, the homeless population disproportionately uses emergency departments of hospitals for medical care. Hospital emergency departments must, by law, serve everybody regardless of ability to pay. According to a study in Hawaii of hospital admissions of homeless people, in one year "1,751 homeless adults were responsible for 564 hospitalizations and $4,000,000 in admissions costs."[2] According to a report in the *New England Journal of Medicine*, when homeless people do enter the hospital, they spend an average of four days longer per visit than nonhomeless people, resulting in extra costs. Without adequate health insurance or access to medical care outside of the emergency departments of hospitals, the cost of medical treatment for homeless individuals will continue to be a drain on communities.

Another area where homelessness proves costly is law enforcement and imprisonment. Laws vary according to municipality, but many common behaviors of homeless people are themselves illegal, such as sleeping in cars, sitting or lying down on sidewalks, soliciting on the streets for money, and urinating or defecating in public. Law enforcement is called upon to enforce these laws, which often results in jail or prison for homeless individuals after repeated offenses. According to research by the Pew Center on the States, the average cost of one month in prison in fiscal year 2010 was $2,593, more expensive than most transitional or permanent housing programs. With laws that target the homeless population and the high costs of imprisonment, homelessness is a drain on law enforcement resources.

The Substance Abuse and Mental Health Services Administration (SAMHSA) reports that approximately 30 percent of people who are chronically homeless have mental health conditions, and 60 percent have experienced mental health problems at some point in their lives. In addition, SAMHSA reports that 80 percent of people who are chronically homeless have experienced drug or alcohol problems at some point, and 50 percent have substance abuse problems along with mental health conditions. This high rate of mental health problems and substance abuse problems is costly with or without treatment. Treatment itself is costly, but failing to fund treatment can lead to costs in other areas—for example, increased emergency room visits or more law enforcement intervention.

Homelessness is a social problem for many reasons. In an era of dwindling state budgets, the economic costs of homelessness are of particular concern. The debate about how spending on homelessness ought to be addressed is just one debate among many surrounding this social issue. A variety of viewpoints on the causes of homelessness, the government programs that aim to help the homeless, and legislation related to homelessness are explored in *Introducing Issues with Opposing Viewpoints: Homelessness.*

Notes
1. Brooke Spellman, Jill Khadduri, Brian Sokol, Josh Leopold, and Abt Associates Inc., "Costs Associated with First-Time Homelessness for Families and Individuals," US Department of Housing and Urban Development, March 2010. www.hud.gov.
2. Senate, Senate Bill No. 2118, Twenty-Sixth Legislature, 2012. www.capitol.hawaii.gov.

Chapter 1

What Are the Causes of Homelessness?

The rate of homelessness in the United States has been made worse by many factors, including a foundering economy.

Homelessness Is a Problem Created by Deregulation and Cutbacks

"We have not used the word 'homelessness' for very long. It is a catch-all term for a host of serious social and economic policy failures."

David Hulchanski

In the following viewpoint David Hulchanski argues that homelessness is a relatively recent social problem in the developed world, caused by cutbacks in social housing programs and an increased reliance on the market to cure social ills. Hulchanski claims that, historically, society has not tolerated the existence of unhoused persons and that the abandonment of a social philosophy that views shelter as a basic need is to blame. Hulchanski is the Dr. Chow Yei Ching Chair in Housing in the Faculty of Social Work at the University of Toronto in Canada.

AS YOU READ, CONSIDER THE FOLLOWING QUESTIONS:

1. According to the author, prior to what decade was it rare to find the term *homelessness* used to describe a social problem?
2. In Canada, according to Hulchanski, social housing units began to be built following the passage of what legislation?
3. The author claims that cutbacks in social housing and related programs began in what year in Canada?

As of late 2009, the English language contained 1 million words, and new words are being added every day. With such abundance in the language, we tend to forget how powerful words can be, and that the names we give to ideas can shape our world view.

Consider a word that we take for granted, but that has far-reaching implications. The word is "homelessness."

The Development of a Social Problem

A search of the *New York Times* historical database covering 1851 to 2005 reveals that it was used in 4,755 articles, but 4,148 of them (87 per cent) were published in the 20 years between 1985 and 2005. Before the 1980s, it is rare to find "homelessness" used to designate a social problem. What happened in that decade that made the difference?

In 1981, the United Nations [UN] announced that 1987 would be the International Year of Shelter for the Homeless. The United Nations wanted to focus on the fact that so many people in less developed countries were unhoused. There was no mention of developed countries like Canada in that 1981 UN resolution.

Moreover, the 1981 UN General Assembly resolution did not use the word "homelessness" because the term as the name of a social problem was not in common use at the time. The 1981 UN resolution was intended to draw attention to the fact that many millions of households in developing countries had no housing. They were unhoused, homeless. They needed adequate housing.

> **FAST FACT**
>
> According to the Canadian Alliance to End Homelessness, although Canada's federal government has estimated that 150,000 Canadians are homeless, other researchers say the number could be as high as 1 million annually.

But by 1987, the focus of the International Year had shifted to include homeless people in the developed nations of the world, including Canada. In that year, several academic and professional conferences focused on the growing number of unhoused people in Canada, not those in developing countries.

The History of the Homeless

Before the 1980s, people in developed countries did not know what it was like to be unhoused. They had housing, even if that housing was in poor condition. Some transient single men in cities were referred to at times as "homeless." But the term had a different meaning then.

For example, in 1960, a report by the Social Planning Council of Metro Toronto called *Homeless and Transient Men*, defined a "homeless man" as one with few or no ties to a family group, who was thus without the economic or social support a family home provides. The men were homeless, not unhoused. They had housing, albeit poor-quality housing—rooming houses or accommodation provided by charities. But they had no home.

Canada at that time thus had homeless individuals, but no problem called "homelessness."

A homeless man collects recyclables in a shopping cart. Many blame rising homelessness on cutbacks in aid and economic deregulation.

The word "homelessness" came into common use in developed countries in the early and mid-1980s to refer to the problem of dehousing—the fact that an increasing number of people who were once housed in these wealthy countries were no longer housed.

Before the 1980s, Canadian urban planners, public health officials, social workers and related professionals had focused on rehousing people into better housing and neighbourhoods.

The Era of Social Housing

During the Depression and World War II, very little new housing was built and many people were living in poor-quality, aging and overcrowded housing. After the war, Canadians revived the housing market, created a functioning mortgage system with government mortgage insurance, built social housing and subsidized private-sector rental housing. About 20,000 social housing units were created every year following the 1973 amendments to the National Housing Act.

In introducing the 1973 housing legislation, the minister of urban affairs—a federal ministry we no longer have today but which existed during most of the 1970s—asserted that our society has an obligation to see that all people are adequately housed.

The minister, Ron Basford, said, "When we talk . . . about the subject of housing, we are talking about an elemental human need—the need for shelter, for physical and emotional comfort in that shelter. When we talk about people's basic needs—the requirements for survival—society and the government obviously have an obligation to assure that these basic needs of shelter are met."

Undoubtedly we would not have the social problem of homelessness today if this philosophy had continued through the 1980s and 1990s to the present day. By the 1980s, however, Canada had a social problem that was and has ever since been called "homelessness."

The New Era of Deregulation

The cutbacks in social housing and related programs began in 1984. In 1993, all federal spending on the construction of new social housing was terminated and in 1996 the federal government further removed itself from low-income housing supply by transferring responsibility for most existing federal social housing to the provinces.

The Threat of Homelessness in Canada

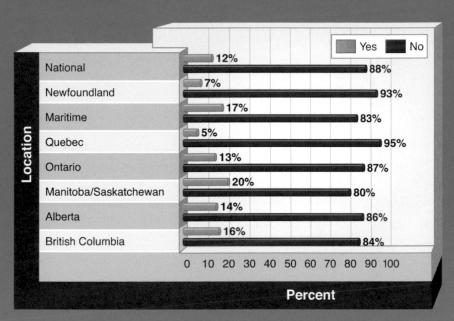

Have you experienced or come close to experiencing homelessness?

Location	Yes	No
National	12%	88%
Newfoundland	7%	93%
Maritime	17%	83%
Quebec	5%	95%
Ontario	13%	87%
Manitoba/Saskatchewan	20%	80%
Alberta	14%	86%
British Columbia	16%	84%

Percent

Taken from: The Strategic Counsel, poll, 2009.

Over the past two decades, we relied on an increasingly deregulated society in which the "genius of market forces" would meet our needs, in which tax cuts, made possible by cuts to programs that largely benefited poor and average-income people, were supposed to "trickle down" to benefit those in need. The competitive economy required, we were told, wage suppression and part-time jobs with no benefits.

By the early 1980s, countries like Canada needed a new term for a new social problem. The word "homelessness" filled the gap. Adding the suffix "-ness" turns the adjective "homeless" into an abstract noun. As such, it allows readers and listeners to imagine whatever they want. It tosses all sorts of problems into one handy term.

In short, we have not used the word "homelessness" for very long. It is a catch-all term for a host of serious social and economic policy failures.

Its widespread usage reflects what has happened to Canadian society—the way we organize who gets what, and our failure to have in place systems for meeting basic human needs in a universal, inclusive fashion.

EVALUATING THE AUTHOR'S ARGUMENTS:

In this viewpoint David Hulchanski argues that the Canadian federal government's termination of low-income housing programs is part of the explanation for a rise in homelessness. What would Charles Johnson, the author of the following viewpoint, say about the decision by the federal government to terminate housing programs?

Homelessness and Urban Poverty Are Created by Government Regulation

Charles Johnson

"While government laws make living on the streets even harder than it already is, government intervention also blocks homeless people's efforts to find themselves shelter outside the conventional housing market."

In the following viewpoint Charles Johnson argues that government antipoverty programs exacerbate urban poverty, preventing people from implementing solutions to help themselves out of poverty, unemployment, and homelessness. Johnson contends that the lack of affordable housing is caused by the very programs meant to address housing shortages, and he proposes that urban homesteading without government regulation is the solution. Johnson is a contributor to *Freeman* magazine and a director and research associate at the Molinari Institute, an organization that promotes market anarchism.

AS YOU READ, CONSIDER THE FOLLOWING QUESTIONS:
  1. According to Johnson, urban poverty is the result of what?
  2. The author claims that what three housing laws drive up housing costs?
  3. According to Johnson, who was responsible for destroying Umoja Village, a homeless homestead site, in 2007?

Governments—local, state, and federal—spend a lot of time wringing their hands about the plight of the urban poor. Look around any government agency and you'll never fail to find some know-it-all with a suit and a nameplate on his desk who has just the right government program to eliminate or ameliorate, or at least contain, the worst aspects of grinding poverty in American cities—especially as experienced by black people, immigrants, people with disabilities, and everyone else marked for the special observation and solicitude of the state bureaucracy. Depending on the bureaucrat's frame of mind, his pet programs might focus on doling out conditional charity to "deserving" poor people, or putting more "at-risk" poor people under the surveillance of social workers and medical experts, or beating up recalcitrant poor people and locking them in cages for several years.

The Impact of Government Programs

But the one thing that the government and its managerial aid workers will never do is just get out of the way and let poor people do the things that poor people naturally do, and always have done, to scratch by.

Government anti-poverty programs are a classic case of the therapeutic state setting out to treat disorders created by the state itself. Urban poverty as we know it is, in fact, exclusively a creature of state intervention in consensual economic dealings. This claim may seem bold, even to most libertarians. But a lot turns on the phrase "as we know it." Even if absolute laissez faire reigned beginning tomorrow, there would still be people in big cities who are living paycheck to paycheck, heavily in debt, homeless, jobless, or otherwise at the bottom rungs of the socioeconomic ladder. These conditions may be persistent social problems, and it may be that free people in a free society will still

have to come up with voluntary institutions and practices for addressing them. But in the state-regimented market that dominates today,
the material predicament that poor people find themselves in—and
the arrangements they must make within that predicament—are bat-
tered into their familiar shape, as if by an invisible fist, through the
diffuse effects of pervasive, interlocking interventions.

Consider the commonplace phenomena of urban poverty.
Livelihoods in American inner cities are typically extremely precari-
ous: as Sudhir Alladi Venkatesh writes in *Off the Books*: "Conditions
in neighborhoods of concentrated poverty can change quickly and in
ways that can leave families unprepared and without much recourse."
Fixed costs of living—rent, food, clothing, and so on—consume most
or all of a family's income, with little or no access to credit, savings,
or insurance to safeguard them from unexpected disasters.

Their poverty often leaves them dependent on other people. It per-
vades the lives of the employed and the unemployed alike: the jobless
fall back on charity or help from family; those who live paycheck to
paycheck, with little chance of finding any work elsewhere, depend
on the good graces of a select few bosses and brokers. One woman
quoted by Venkatesh explained why she continued to work through
an exploitative labor shark rather than leaving for a steady job with a
well-to-do family: "And what if that family gets rid of me? Where am
I going next? See, I can't take that chance, you know. . . . All I got is
Johnnie and it took me the longest just to get him on my side."

A Better Solution to Poverty

The daily experience of the urban poor is shaped by geographical
concentration in socially and culturally isolated ghetto neighborhoods within the larger city, which have their own characteristic features: housing is concentrated in dilapidated apartments and housing
projects, owned by a select few absentee landlords; many abandoned
buildings and vacant lots are scattered through the neighborhood,
which remain unused for years at a time; the use of outside spaces is
affected by large numbers of unemployed or homeless people.

The favorite solutions of the welfare state—government doles and
"urban renewal" projects—mark no real improvement. Rather than
freeing poor people from dependence on benefactors and bosses, they

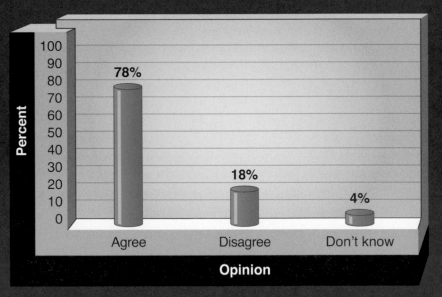

Do you agree or disagree with the following statement...

"There should be less government regulation of how people make daily choices in their lives and jobs."

Taken from: Clarus Research Group, October 19–20, 2011.

merely transfer the dependence to the state, leaving the least politically connected people at the mercy of the political process.

But in a free market—a truly free market, where individual poor people are just as free as established formal-economy players to use their own property, their own labor, their own know-how, and the resources that are available to them—the informal, enterprising actions by poor people themselves would do far more to systematically undermine, or completely eliminate, each of the stereotypical conditions that welfare statists deplore. Every day and in every culture from time out of mind, poor people have repeatedly shown remarkable intelligence, courage, persistence, and creativity in finding ways to put food on the table, save money, keep safe, raise families, live full lives, learn, enjoy themselves, and experience beauty, whenever, wherever, and to whatever degree they have been free to do so. The fault for despairing, dilapidated urban ghettoes lies not in the pressures of the market, nor in the character flaws of individual poor people, nor in the characteristics of ghetto subcultures. The fault lies in the state and its persistent interference with poor people's own efforts to get by through independent work, clever hustling, scratching together resources, and voluntary mutual aid.

The So-Called Housing Crisis

Progressives routinely deplore the "affordable housing crisis" in American cities. In cities such as New York and Los Angeles, about 20 to 25 percent of low-income renters are spending more than half their incomes just on housing. But it is the very laws that Progressives favor—land-use policies, zoning codes, and building codes—that ratchet up housing costs, stand in the way of alternative housing options, and confine poor people to ghetto neighborhoods. Historically, when they have been free to do so, poor people have happily disregarded the ideals of political humanitarians and found their own ways to cut housing costs, even in bustling cities with tight housing markets.

One way was to get other families, or friends, or strangers, to move in and split the rent. Depending on the number of people sharing a home, this might mean a less-comfortable living situation; it might even mean one that is unhealthy. But decisions about health and comfort are best made by the individual people who bear the costs and reap the benefits. Unfortunately today the decisions are made ahead of time by city governments through zoning laws that prohibit or restrict sharing a home among people not related by blood or marriage, and building codes that limit the number of residents in a building.

Those who cannot make enough money to cover the rent on their own, and cannot split the rent enough due to zoning and building codes, are priced out of the housing market entirely. Once homeless, they are left exposed not only to the elements, but also to harassment or arrest by the police for "loitering" or "vagrancy," even on public property, in efforts to force them into overcrowded and dangerous institutional shelters. But while government laws make living on the streets even harder than it already is, government intervention also blocks homeless people's efforts to find themselves shelter outside the conventional housing market. One of the oldest and commonest survival strategies practiced by the urban poor is to find wild or abandoned land and build shanties on it out of salvageable scrap materials. Scrap materials are plentiful, and large portions of land in ghetto neighborhoods are typically left unused as condemned buildings or vacant lots. Formal title is very often seized by the city government or by quasi-governmental "development" corporations through the use of eminent domain. Lots are held out of use, often for years at a time, while they await government public-works projects or developers willing to buy up the land for large-scale building.

The Urban Homesteading Solution

In a free market, vacant lots and abandoned buildings could eventually be homesteaded by anyone willing to do the work of occupying and using them. Poor people could use abandoned spaces within their own communities for setting up shop, for gardening, or for living space. In Miami, in October 2006, a group of community organizers and about 35 homeless people built Umoja Village, a shanty town, on an inner-city lot that the local government had kept vacant for years. They publicly stated to the local government that "We have only one demand . . . leave us alone."

FAST FACT

In the late nineteenth century and early twentieth century, several US homestead acts allowed people to settle on land and file for ownership as long as they used and improved the land.

That would be the end of the story in a free market: there would be no eminent domain, no government ownership, and thus also no political process of seizure and redevelopment; once-homeless people could establish property rights to abandoned land through their own sweat equity—without fear of the government's demolishing their work and selling their land out from under them. But back in Miami, the city attorney and city council took about a month to begin legal efforts to destroy the residents' homes and force them off the lot. In April 2007 the city police took advan-

In Kansas City, Missouri, residents have transformed slum properties by creating gardens and rehabbing homes as part of an urban homesteading project. Such projects are often thwarted by the very government programs intended to relieve urban poverty.

tage of an accidental fire to enforce its politically fabricated title to the land, clearing the lot, arresting 11 people, and erecting a fence to safeguard the once-again vacant lot for professional "affordable housing" developers.

Had the city government not made use of its supposed title to the abandoned land, it no doubt could have made use of state and federal building codes to ensure that residents would be forced back into homelessness—for their own safety, of course. That is in fact what a county health commission in Indiana did to a 93-year-old man named Thelmon Green, who lived in his '86 Chevrolet van, which the local towing company allowed him to keep on its lot. Many people thrown into poverty by a sudden financial catastrophe live out of a car for weeks or months until they get back on their feet. Living in a car is cramped, but it beats living on the streets: a car means a place you can have to yourself, which holds your possessions, with doors you can lock, and sometimes even air conditioning and heating. But staying in a car over the long term is much harder to manage without running afoul of the law. Thelmon Green got by well enough in his van for ten years, but when the *Indianapolis Star* printed a human-interest story on him last December, the county health commission took notice and promptly ordered Green evicted from his own van, in the name of the local housing code.

Since government housing codes impose detailed requirements on the size, architecture, and building materials for new permanent housing, as well as on specialized and extremely expensive contract work for electricity, plumbing, and other luxuries, they effectively obstruct or destroy most efforts to create transitional, intermediate, or informal sorts of shelter that cost less than rented space in government-approved housing projects, but provide more safety and comfort than living on the street.

EVALUATING THE AUTHOR'S ARGUMENTS:

In this viewpoint Charles Johnson claims that it is up to individual people to decide whether or not their living situation is healthy. What is the argument for the opposing view that favors government regulation?

The Economic Recession Has Sparked an Increase in Homelessness

"The recession has widened the continuum of distress that undergirds modern homelessness."

Michelle Chen

In the following viewpoint Michelle Chen argues that the recent recession has left many Americans homeless or on the brink of homelessness. Chen claims that part of the problem is the lack of any safety net that buffers against economic emergencies. She contends that most of the homeless are unemployed but face many obstacles in finding and maintaining employment, including the obstacle of being homeless. Chen is a contributing editor at *In These Times* and associate editor at *CultureStrike*.

AS YOU READ, CONSIDER THE FOLLOWING QUESTIONS:

1. According to the author, New York City has seen what percentage of growth in the homeless population since fiscal year 2002?
2. Chen claims that approximately what fraction of the homeless are employed?
3. What four factors does the author attribute to the underlying system of modern homelessness?

For millions of American households, the recession has turned the once unthinkable into inescapable reality: suddenly finding themselves out of a job, then falling behind on the rent, and finally, losing everything.

New York City's exploding homelessness crisis is a case study in how new forms of hardship are reshaping the country's social landscape.

The New York City Coalition for the Homeless reports that on any given night, 39,000 New Yorkers are huddled in city shelters. Though urban homelessness is typically associated with chronic drug users or the mentally ill, New York's homeless now include some 10,000 families, with more than 16,500 children.

The trend marks a 45-percent growth in the homeless population since fiscal year 2002, despite Mayor Michael Bloomberg's high-profile efforts to revamp the shelter system.

While previous downturns have been more severe overall, the coalition says "the current year is the worst on record for New York City homelessness since the Great Depression of the 1930s."

Yet the shelter numbers are just a crude snapshot of the scourge. Many homeless people see shelters as so inhospitable that they opt

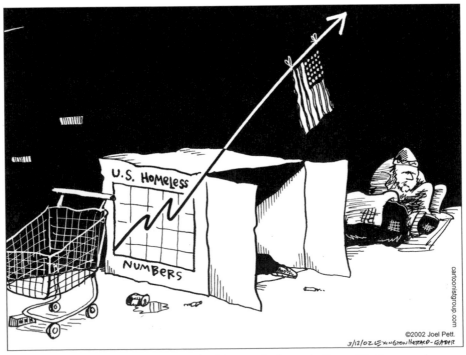

for the streets instead. And many may be overlooked in official tallies because they are "doubled up" with friends or relatives. Often, children must turn to schools, not shelters, as the closest thing to home, clinging to school-based aid programs as their parents struggle for stability.

And then there are those for whom homelessness is just one overdue bill away—the families who are cleaning out the shelves at food pantries to juggle overwhelming debts. A recent national survey of food banks by Feeding America found a safety net in tatters:

FAST FACT

As of August 2012 the New York City Coalition for the Homeless reports that 44,400 people are in New York City shelters, including 18,000 children.

> 99 percent of all participating food banks reported a significant surge in demand for emergency food assistance over the past year . . . the increase is particularly driven by first-time users of the food assistance system (98 percent of food banks) and more people who have recently lost their jobs (92 percent).

If you have trouble imagining the trauma and humiliation of not having a roof over your head, so do many of the homeless, at first: formerly middle-class parents may be stunned that they're choosing tonight between sleeping in a car or piling into a motel room, or skipping a few meals to pay for their kids' school supplies.

The *Washington Post*'s profile of the Vasquez family in Virginia, who moved from a comfortable townhouse to a shelter, reveals a shock of disbelief in the face of sudden poverty:

> At the shelter, every space is shared: the television room, the playground, the dining room that resembles a school cafeteria. To hold hands in the bedroom where the five members of the family sleep, Yolanda and Ron must reach across the gap between their beds.

> During any other time, the Vazquez family's experience might seem an extreme example. But area shelters report that since the recession started, they've seen schoolteachers, computer technicians and interior designers walk through their doors.

So more working Americans are watching the economic security they once took for granted crumble faster than they can comprehend. The Homeless Employment Survey, conducted by the Sacramento Ending Chronic Homeless Initiative, indicates that the vast majority of those surveyed were unemployed but wanted to work. And one in ten were actually working while homeless.

Among the top barriers to employment were a lack of skills, education or training, as well as disability or health issues. And yet this was not an unskilled population: "About one-third stated they had computer [33.5%]; hospitality [32.8%]; construction [32.2%] and retail skills [29.1%]."

Many cited homelessness itself as the biggest obstacle to holding down a job.

That tragic catch-22 seems to be playing out in New York City. Advocates say that due to time limits and other constraints on housing assistance, the social service system ironically ends up hindering homeless families from working toward self-sufficiency.

A homeless family tries to stay warm outside the shelter where they live. The New York City Coalition for the Homeless reports that on any given night ten thousand families, including 16,500 children, are homeless.

The recession has widened the continuum of distress that undergirds modern homelessness: the economic vulnerability bred by a lack of affordable housing, limited educational opportunities, a broken healthcare system, and weak community infrastructure. Though the federal stimulus provided some emergency homeless assistance, lawmakers haven't owned up to the problem as an entrenched social crisis. The sense of denial felt by some of today's newly homeless reflects the willful ignorance of Washington.

Homelessness maybe the extreme end of the recession, but it's closer than you may think. If this recession has taught us anything, it's that while we're increasingly divided by inequality, we're also leveled by common hardships in ways we never imagined before.

EVALUATING THE AUTHOR'S ARGUMENTS:

In this viewpoint Michelle Chen claims that the social service system can end up hindering the homeless from achieving self-sufficiency. For this reason, do you think she would agree with Charles Johnson that government programs should be eliminated? Why or why not?

A Change in Federal Policy Is the Ultimate Cause of Increased Homelessness

"While the recession has swollen the ranks of the homeless population, modern homelessness has been with us for more than a quarter-century."

Lizzy Ratner and Patrick Markee

In the following viewpoint Lizzy Ratner and Patrick Markee argue that although the recent economic recession has increased the number of homeless people, homelessness has been a problem since former president Ronald Reagan's administration changed federal housing policy. Ratner and Markee claim that the elimination of federal housing programs and reliance on the free market is the ultimate cause of the recent rise in homelessness and can only be addressed by a reversal in federal policy. Ratner is a journalist, and Markee is a senior policy analyst at the Coalition for the Homeless in New York City and a member of the board of directors of the National Coalition for the Homeless.

Lizzy Ratner and Patrick Markee, "Hope for the Homeless?" *The Nation*, vol. 288, no. 5, February 9, 2009, p. 16. Copyright © 2009 by The Nation. Reprinted with permission from the February 9, 2009 issue of The Nation. For subscription information, call 1-800-333-8536. Portions of each week's *Nation* magazine can be accessed at http://www.thenation.com.

1. According to the authors, how many homeless students are there in California?
2. Ratner and Markee claim that funding for affordable housing programs by the federal government has declined by how much since 2004?
3. The authors claim that academic research shows that the best way to solve homelessness is to do what?

On January 14, [2009] as the combined forces of recession and foreclosure continued their long, cruel assault on the Rust Belt, Cleveland's public school system marked the new semester with a troubling piece of data: the number of students who had been homeless at some point during the school year had jumped to 1,728. Compared with the same date in 2006, this number represented a spike of nearly 150 percent and served as further confirmation that, for all the [whining] of Wall Street executives, the poor and vulnerable have been hardest hit by the flailing economy. Not that Cleveland's poorest students needed reminding. In December [2008], when Project ACT, a social service program for homeless students run by the Cleveland Metropolitan School District, asked a group of homeless parents what they wanted for Christmas, the parents responded with wish lists worthy of [Charles Dickens's] *Little Dorrit*: toilet paper, bleach, paper towels, food.

"We figured they'd be asking for some nice things, [but] they were asking for basic, basic household things," said Marcia Zashin, Project ACT's director. "Times are tough. They're very tough."

An Epidemic of Homelessness

Such are the stories pouring out of schools and homeless shelters these days, evidence of a crisis that many fear is bound to get worse. Throughout the country, homelessness is rising, with ever more families in ever more towns and cities sleeping in shelters, surfing friends' couches and camping in their cars. In San Bernardino, California, for instance, the City Unified School District counted roughly one-third more homeless students in the 2007–08 school year than in the

Many of today's homeless are renters who paid their rent but were evicted because their landlords were unable to make their mortgage payments. Some blame a change in federal housing policy dating back to the Ronald Reagan administration.

previous one, part of a stomach-churning trend that has pushed the number of homeless students in the state past 224,000, according to local officials. In Boston the number of families without homes shot up 22 percent, from 3,175 in December 2007 to 3,870 in December 2008. And in New York City, which shelters an astonishing 36,000 homeless people each night (including nearly 16,000 kids), the number of newly homeless families entering the shelter system hit an all-time high in autumn, with the influx in November 44 percent higher than the previous year. Along the way, the total number of homeless families bedding down each night in shelters topped 9,700—the highest number since the city began keeping records more than twenty-five years ago.

By most accounts, there's little mystery to this rise in the ranks of shelter seekers. It's the economy and, more specifically, the recession and the foreclosure crisis. As people have lost their paychecks, or as the homes they were renting were foreclosed—most of today's homeless foreclosure victims are renters who were evicted, even though they paid rent, because their landlord had not kept up with the mortgage—their tenuous grip on stability has slipped away. And many housing experts think this could be just the beginning. Because the recession is far from over; because the unemployment rate hit 7.2 percent in December [2008] and is expected to climb; because the foreclosure crisis has more misery to dole out; and because homelessness is a lagging indicator—families tend to cling to their homes as long as they can, forgoing food, clothes and medication just to keep their roof—the number of homeless families will likely continue to spike.

But there's another essential point, one that bears fundamentally on how we understand—and tackle—this crisis. While the recession has swollen the ranks of the homeless population, modern homelessness has been with us for more than a quarter-century. Long before subprime mortgages, credit default swaps and the most recent stock market crash, the United States was in the grip of the longest period of sustained mass homelessness since the Great Depression. Indeed, even before the current economic downturn some 3.5 million Americans (including 1.4 million children) experienced homelessness during the course of a year. For this we can thank not a periodic dip in the business cycle but an affordable-housing crunch spawned by nearly three decades of slash-and-burn housing policy.

Changes in Federal Housing Policy

Just as the Wall Street meltdown can be traced to the deregulate-at-any-cost ideology of the [former president Ronald] Reagan years, modern homelessness and the widening housing affordability gap were fostered in the Gipper's [Reagan's] free-market nursery. From the earliest days of his administration, Reagan set about systematically dismantling federal housing programs, slashing funds for federal rental vouchers and public housing. He also initiated the shift in federal low-income housing policy away from subsidized development to tax-credit programs, which fail to help the poorest families. The reason was pure conservative hocus-pocus: the idea that housing is a commodity best created and priced by the unregulated, unfettered market and that government should play little or no role in guaranteeing shelter to its poorest citizens.

During the next decades, this ideology never disappeared, and it enjoyed a particularly virulent renaissance in [former president] George W. Bush's America. Even as the Bush administration made a show of doling out small increases to the homeless services budget (though never enough to meet the need), it hacked away at public housing, Section 8 vouchers and other housing programs, undermining any attempt at reducing family homelessness. Indeed, since 2004 funding for affordable housing programs has declined by $2.2 billion. The result is a country in which only one in four eligible low-income households receives federal housing assistance while those forced to go it alone, without any government assistance, face an increasingly harsh landscape of rising rents and declining wages. It's no wonder the number of poor renters paying more than half their income for rent rose by more than 1 million households, or 29 percent, between 2001 and 2007.

Fortunately, we have a chance to rewire the country's housing policy, an opportunity born of the start of [President] Barack Obama's administration and a climate made more receptive to public investment by the awful imperatives of the economic meltdown. More than at any time in recent history, this moment calls for the kind of visionary and dramatic action too rarely seen from leaders—certainly not Republicans but also many Democrats, who have spent much of the past two decades fidgeting on the margins of federal housing programs.

Toward Ending Homelessness

There are a lot of ways President Obama could begin tackling such a challenge—including a bold and unequivocal commitment to ending homelessness once and for all. As another critical first step, the Obama team (including New York City housing commissioner Shaun Donovan, who is expected to be confirmed as the new head of the Department of Housing and Urban Development [assumed office

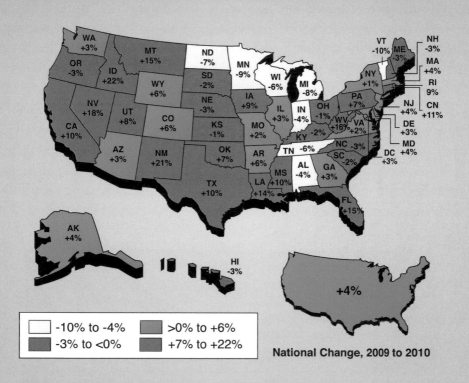

Changes in Unemployed People, 2009 to 2010

WA +3%
OR -3%
ID +22%
MT +15%
ND -7%
MN -9%
WI -6%
MI -8%
VT -10%
NH -3%
ME -3%
MA +4%
NY +1%
RI 9%
SD -2%
WY +6%
NE -3%
IA +9%
PA +7%
NJ +4%
CN +11%
NV +18%
UT +8%
CO +6%
IL +3%
IN -4%
OH -1%
WV +16%
VA +2%
DE +3%
CA +10%
KS -1%
MO +2%
KY -2%
MD
AZ +3%
NM +21%
OK +7%
AR +6%
TN -6%
NC -3%
DC +4%
SC -2%
TX +10%
LA +14%
MS +10%
AL -4%
GA +3%
FL +15%
AK +4%
HI -3%

☐ -10% to -4%	■ >0% to +6%
■ -3% to <0%	■ +7% to +22%

+4%

National Change, 2009 to 2010

Taken from: National Alliance to End Homelessness and Homelessness Research Institute. "The State of Homelessness in America 2012," January 2012. www.endhomelessness.org.

January 26, 2009]) and Congress can adopt a $45 billion proposal, drafted by the National Low Income Housing Coalition and forty other progressive policy groups, as part of the stimulus package. This plan is premised on years of academic research: that the best way to solve homelessness is to provide people with homes—to create permanent supportive housing (i.e., affordable housing with support services) for people living with mental illness and other special needs and to offer affordable housing assistance (in the form of vouchers or low-income housing) to homeless families.

Toward this end, the plan calls for a minimum of 400,000 new rental vouchers as well as a $10 billion infusion over two years in the recently created National Housing Trust Fund—a move that would jump-start construction of badly needed low-cost homes. To help address more imminent needs, the plan suggests expanded aid for victims of foreclosures and another $2 billion for vital homelessness prevention services. Additional investments of $15.4 billion would address the long-neglected upkeep of public housing and help these and other subsidized developments "go green" by improving energy efficiency. Taken together, these initiatives will help more than 800,000 vulnerable households and create more than 200,000 jobs.

Of course, cleaning up the wreckage of three decades of failed federal housing policy will take more than one stimulus; these measures are just the beginning of what's needed. But if change is the order of the day, dismantling the Reagan-Bush legacy of modern homelessness would be a promising way to start.

EVALUATING THE AUTHORS' ARGUMENTS:

In this viewpoint Lizzy Ratner and Patrick Markee argue that homelessness is ultimately caused by a change in federal policy. Does the authors' viewpoint align more with David Hulchanski's or Charles Johnson's viewpoint from earlier in this chapter? Explain.

Increased Poverty Has Caused an Increase in Shared Households

Laryssa Mykyta and Suzanne Macartney

"Household sharing reduced the total number of additional adults who would have been classified as poor except for the income of other family members in the household."

In the following viewpoint Laryssa Mykyta and Suzanne Macartney argue that the increase in shared households between 2007 and 2010 is part of a strategy to pool resources to cope with economic vulnerability. Mykyta and Macartney cite statistics that show people in shared households have higher personal poverty rates than others but lower household poverty rates, which is consistent with their theory that sharing households is a strategy to avoid poverty. Mykyta and Macartney are analysts in the US Census Bureau's Poverty Statistics Branch. Mykyta is also coauthor of *Raise the Floor: Wages and Policies That Work for All of Us*.

Laryssa Mykyta and Suzanne Macartney, "Sharing a Household: Household Composition and Economic Well-Being: 2007–2010," US Census Bureau, June 2012, pp. 2–3, 5–8.

AS YOU READ, CONSIDER THE FOLLOWING QUESTIONS:
1. According to the authors, by how much did the percentage of shared households grow from 2007 to 2010?
2. In 2010 personal poverty among those in shared households was how much higher than those not in shared households, according to the authors?
3. According to Mykyta and Macartney, what percentage of the increase in additional adults in shared households between 2007 and 2010 occurred among those aged twenty-five to thirty-four?

A mong adults, 27.7 percent resided in shared households in spring 2007. By spring 2010, 30.1 percent of all adults lived in shared households.

An Increase in Shared Households

Shared households are occupied by both primary adults and additional adults. Primary adults are householders and their spouses or cohabiting partners. The number of primary adults who shared their households increased by 12.1 percent between 2007 and 2010. In contrast, the number of primary adults not living in shared households fell 0.9 percent over this period.

A subset of persons in shared households is "additional adults." Additional adults are persons aged 18 and older not enrolled in school who are not householders, the spouses, nor the cohabiting partners of householders. Additional adults may be relatives or nonrelatives of the householder. Additional adults include adult children who live with their parents, as well as parents who live in their children's households. The definition of additional adults also includes roommates, housemates, or boarders.

Additional adults accounted for 13.9 percent of all adults in spring 2007. By spring 2010, the share of additional adults increased to 15.0 percent of adults. The adult population increased by 2.9 percent, while the number of additional adults increased by 11.1 percent over the 2007 to 2010 period.

Being an additional adult in someone else's household was a common living arrangement in 2010 among those aged 18 to 24. Some young adults lived with their parents, while others shared dwellings with one or more roommates. The number of additional adults among those aged 18 to 24 increased by 5.9 percent between 2007 and 2010.

Household sharing was not limited to the youngest adults. The number of adults aged 25 to 34 who lived in someone else's household increased by 18.1 percent, while the number aged 35 to 64 increased by 9.7 percent between 2007 and 2010. The 1.5 million increase in the number of additional adults aged 25 to 34 accounted for about 45 percent of the total increase in additional adults during the period. . . .

Poverty in Shared Households

It is difficult to assess the precise impact of household sharing on economic well-being, but the constructed measures of poverty based on personal income and total household income provide some evidence. . . .

For householders heading shared households, both official and household poverty rates for 2010 were lower than for other householders. This

Members of a communal farm share dinner together. Bad economic times have forced many families to share households.

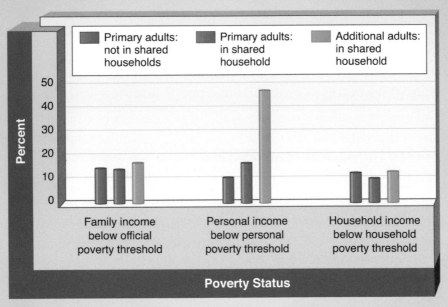

Official, Personal, and Household Poverty Status for Adults by Shared Household Status, 2010

Legend:
- Primary adults: not in shared households
- Primary adults: in shared household
- Additional adults: in shared household

Y-axis: Percent (0, 10, 20, 30, 40, 50)

X-axis (Poverty Status):
- Family income below official poverty threshold
- Personal income below personal poverty threshold
- Household income below household poverty threshold

Taken from: Current Population Survey, Annual Social and Economic Supplement, 2011. Laryssa Mykyta and Suzanne Macartney. "Sharing a Household: Household Composition and Economic Well-Being, 2007–2010." US Census Bureau, June 2012. www.census.gov.

contrasts with personal poverty rates. Personal poverty was higher for householders in shared households than for householders who were not in shared households (8.2 percentage points higher in 2010). Higher personal poverty rates for those heading shared households suggests that this group has fewer individual resources than their counterparts. However, lower official and household poverty rates among householders heading shared households suggest that household sharing lessened economic strain.

Additional adults aged 25 and older had an official poverty rate of 14.6 percent in 2010. Had poverty status been determined by personal income, 40.7 percent of additional adults aged 25 and older would have been poor in 2010. In addition, the official poverty rate for young adults aged 25 to 34 living with parents was 8.4 percent in 2010, but if poverty status was determined by personal income, 45.3 percent would have been in poverty.

A Strategy to Pool Resources

Consistent with the understanding of household sharing as a strategy to pool resources, additional adults had higher personal poverty rates compared with primary adults in both 2007 and 2010. Official poverty rates were also higher among additional adults than among primary adults in both years. However, household poverty rates were not significantly different between additional and primary adults in either year.

In addition, among persons aged 25 and older, there was no statistical difference in household poverty rates between primary adults, compared with additional adults. However, official poverty rates and personal poverty rates were higher among additional adults than for primary adults aged 25 and older.

Official poverty rates and personal poverty rates increased for members of both shared and nonshared households between the pre- and post-recession years. However, the magnitude of the increase in official poverty rates and in personal poverty rates did not differ significantly among householders in shared households and householders who did not share their households. In contrast, family and personal poverty rates increased to a greater degree for additional adults than for primary adults. For example, among additional adults aged 25 and older, the personal poverty rate increased 5.1 percentage points between 2007 and 2010, compared with 1.2 percentage points for primary adults. However, the change in *household poverty rates* between 2007 and 2010 was not significantly different for primary adults and additional adults. . . .

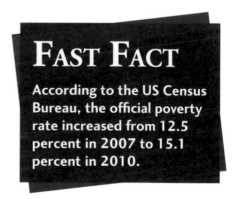

FAST FACT

According to the US Census Bureau, the official poverty rate increased from 12.5 percent in 2007 to 15.1 percent in 2010.

Household sharing reduced the total number of additional adults who would have been classified as poor except for the income of other family members in the household. A total of 8.7 million persons in 2007, and 10.5 million persons in 2010, would have been classified as poor solely on the basis of individual income. Looking only at additional adults aged 25 and older, household sharing reduced the number who would have been classified as poor based on their own resources by 5.6 million in 2007 and 6.7 million in 2010.

Economic Vulnerability in Shared Households

In the United States, the number and percentage of shared households and the number and percentage of adults in shared households increased over the course of the recession which began in December of 2007 and ended in June 2009. By 2010, 22.0 million residences were shared, 18.7 percent of all households.

Consistent with the increase in shared households from 2007 to 2010, the number of persons living in shared households also increased. Additional adults in shared households (not householders, their spouses, or cohabiting partners) increased and accounted for 15.0 percent of all adults by 2010. More than one-half of additional adults were young (under age 35). Yet nearly one-half of the increase in the number of additional adults over the course of the recession (45 percent) occurred among those aged 25 to 34. Additional adults were more likely to live with relatives than unrelated householders. More than 45 percent of all additional adults in 2010 lived with their parents.

Most importantly, official poverty and the constructed household poverty measure were lower among householders in shared households. This suggests bringing additional adults into the household may have been a strategy to mitigate challenging economic circumstances. Results also suggest economically vulnerable householders were more likely to share households than their more advantaged counterparts. Personal poverty rates were higher for householders heading shared households than for other householders. The outcome counters the notion that economically stable householders typically take in more economically strapped family and friends.

Household sharing seems to be a means of alleviating economic strain at the household level. When resources were combined across members, household poverty rates were lower for shared households than for other households. Although the recession reduced income and increased poverty for many adults, the effects were generally worse for additional adults in someone else's household than for others. Compared to householders and their spouses or partners, additional adults were more economically vulnerable with higher official and personal poverty rates.

EVALUATING THE AUTHORS' ARGUMENTS:

In this viewpoint Laryssa Mykyta and Suzanne Macartney argue that an increase in shared households is the result of economic insecurity. Do you think the increase in shared households is something to be concerned about? Why or why not?

The Problems of Poverty and Substandard Housing Are Overstated

Robert Rector and Rachel Sheffield

"By their own reports, the average poor person had sufficient funds to meet all essential needs and to obtain medical care for family members throughout the year whenever needed."

In the following viewpoint Robert Rector and Rachel Sheffield argue that the so-called poor in America actually face few hardships. Rector and Sheffield claim that those who qualify as poor overwhelmingly possess luxury possessions, have plenty to eat, and have housing that is more than adequate. The authors contend that periodic hardships for the poor are a reality and need to be addressed, but they conclude that most of these hardships are temporary. Rector is a senior research fellow and Sheffield a research associate at the Heritage Foundation.

AS YOU READ, CONSIDER THE FOLLOWING QUESTIONS:
1. According to Rector and Sheffield, what fraction of the poor, as defined by the US Census Bureau, have cable or satellite TV?
2. What percentage of the homeless own their own homes, according to the authors?
3. The authors claim that, among the poor, how many out of twenty-five will become temporarily homeless during the year?

Today [September 13, 2011], the Census Bureau released its annual poverty report, which declared that a record 46.2 million (roughly one in seven) Americans were poor in 2010. The numbers were up sharply from the previous year's total of 43.6 million. Although the current recession has greatly increased the numbers of the poor, high levels of poverty predate the recession. In most years for the past two decades, the Census Bureau has declared that at least 35 million Americans lived in poverty.

Facts About the Poor

However, understanding poverty in America requires looking behind these numbers at the actual living conditions of the individuals the government deems to be poor. For most Americans, the word "poverty" suggests near destitution: an inability to provide nutritious food, clothing, and reasonable shelter for one's family. But only a small number of the 46 million persons classified as "poor" by the Census Bureau fit that description. While real material hardship certainly does occur, it is limited in scope and severity.

The following are facts about persons defined as "poor" by the Census Bureau as taken from various government reports:

- 80 percent of poor households have air conditioning. In 1970, only 36 percent of the entire U.S. population enjoyed air conditioning.
- 92 percent of poor households have a microwave.
- Nearly three-fourths have a car or truck, and 31 percent have two or more cars or trucks.
- Nearly two-thirds have cable or satellite TV.

- Two-thirds have at least one DVD player, and 70 percent have a VCR.
- Half have a personal computer, and one in seven have two or more computers.
- More than half of poor families with children have a video game system, such as an Xbox or PlayStation.
- 43 percent have Internet access.
- One-third have a wide-screen plasma or LCD TV.
- One-fourth have a digital video recorder system, such as a TiVo.

For decades, the living conditions of the poor have steadily improved. Consumer items that were luxuries or significant purchases for the middle class a few decades ago have become commonplace in poor households, partially because of the normal downward price trend that follows introduction of a new product.

Newly built and rebuilt houses for the poor stand next to each other on a Washington, DC, street. Some policy experts point out that the US poor are much better off than the poor in other countries.

Unsubstantiated Claims About the Poor

Liberals use the declining relative prices of many amenities to argue that it is no big deal that poor households have air conditioning, computers, cable TV, and wide-screen TV. They contend, polemically, that even though most poor families may have a house full of modern conveniences, the average poor family still suffers from substantial deprivation in basic needs, such as food and housing. In reality, this is just not true.

Although the mainstream media broadcast alarming stories about widespread and severe hunger in the nation, in reality, most of the poor do not experience hunger or food shortages. The U.S. Department of Agriculture collects data on these topics in its household food security survey. For 2009, the survey showed:

> **FAST FACT**
>
> In 2010 the US Census Bureau defined poverty for a family of four as having less income than $22,314, excluding any welfare assistance.

- 96 percent of poor parents stated that their children were never hungry at any time during the year because they could not afford food.
- 83 percent of poor families reported having enough food to eat.
- 82 percent of poor adults reported never being hungry at any time in the prior year due to lack of money for food.

Other government surveys show that the average consumption of protein, vitamins, and minerals is virtually the same for poor and middle-class children and is well above recommended norms in most cases.

The Housing Situation of the Poor

Television newscasts about poverty in America generally portray the poor as homeless people or as a destitute family living in an overcrowded, dilapidated trailer. In fact, however:

- Over the course of a year, 4 percent of poor persons become temporarily homeless.
- Only 9.5 percent of the poor live in mobile homes or trailers, 49.5 percent live in separate single-family houses or townhouses, and 40 percent live in apartments.
- 42 percent of poor households actually own their own homes.
- Only 6 percent of poor households are over-crowded. More than two-thirds have more than two rooms per person.
- The average poor American has more living space than the typical non-poor person in Sweden, France, or the United Kingdom.

- The vast majority of the homes or apartments of the poor are in good repair.

By their own reports, the average poor person had sufficient funds to meet all essential needs and to obtain medical care for family members throughout the year.

Of course, poor Americans do not live in the lap of luxury. The poor clearly struggle to make ends meet, but they are generally struggling to pay for cable TV, air conditioning, and a car, as well as for food on the table. The average poor person is far from affluent, but his lifestyle is far from the images of stark deprivation purveyed equally by advocacy groups and the media.

The Infrequent Hardships of the Poor

The fact that the average poor household has many modern conveniences and experiences no substantial hardships does not mean that no families face hardships. As noted, the overwhelming majority of the poor are well housed and not over-crowded, but one in 25 will become temporarily homeless during the year. While most of the poor have a sufficient and fairly steady supply of food, one in five poor adults will experience temporary food shortages and hunger at some point in a year.

The poor man who has lost his home or suffers intermittent hunger will find no consolation in the fact that his condition occurs infrequently in American society. His hardships are real and must be an

Percentage of Poor US Households That Have Various Amenities

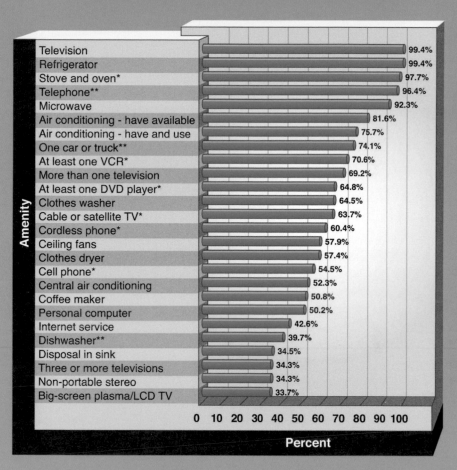

Amenity	Percent
Television	99.4%
Refrigerator	99.4%
Stove and oven*	97.7%
Telephone**	96.4%
Microwave	92.3%
Air conditioning - have available	81.6%
Air conditioning - have and use	75.7%
One car or truck**	74.1%
At least one VCR*	70.6%
More than one television	69.2%
At least one DVD player*	64.8%
Clothes washer	64.5%
Cable or satellite TV*	63.7%
Cordless phone*	60.4%
Ceiling fans	57.9%
Clothes dryer	57.4%
Cell phone*	54.5%
Central air conditioning	52.3%
Coffee maker	50.8%
Personal computer	50.2%
Internet service	42.6%
Dishwasher**	39.7%
Disposal in sink	34.5%
Three or more televisions	34.3%
Non-portable stereo	34.3%
Big-screen plasma/LCD TV	33.7%

*Residential Energy Consumption Survey of 2005
**American Housing Survey of 2009

Taken from: Unless noted otherwise figures are from the US Department of Energy, Residential Energy Consumption Survey 2009. Robert Rector and Rachel Sheffield. "Understanding Poverty in the United States: Surprising Facts About America's Poor." *Backgrounder*, no. 2607, September 13, 2011. www.heritage.org.

important concern for policymakers. Nonetheless, anti-poverty policy needs to be based on accurate information. Gross exaggeration of the extent and severity of hardships in America will not benefit society, the taxpayers, or the poor.

Finally, welfare policy needs to address the causes of poverty, not merely the symptoms. Among families with children, the collapse of marriage and erosion of the work ethic are the principal long-term causes of poverty. When the recession ends, welfare policy must require able-bodied recipients to work or prepare for work as a condition of receiving aid. It should also strengthen marriage in low-income communities rather than ignore and penalize it.

EVALUATING THE AUTHORS' ARGUMENTS:

In this viewpoint Robert Rector and Rachel Sheffield question a definition of poverty that allows for the possession of luxury products and adequate housing and food. According to what they say in the viewpoint, what would their proposed definition of poverty entail?

Chapter 2

What Government Programs Work to Help the Homeless?

Volunteers unload food at a local food shelf. The federal government subsidizes many such organizations.

Viewpoint

1

A Housing-First Strategy Works to Decrease Homelessness

The Christian Science Monitor

In the following viewpoint the *Christian Science Monitor* argues that current statistics support the need to continue the push to end homelessness through use of a housing-first strategy. The *Christian Science Monitor* claims that giving homeless people housing first and then following up with services has proved to be an effective method of ending homelessness, as the decrease in the number of chronically homeless illustrates. Nonetheless, the author claims that the rise in the number of temporarily homeless shows the need for further efforts. *The Christian Science Monitor* is a national newspaper.

AS YOU READ, CONSIDER THE FOLLOWING QUESTIONS:

1. By what percentage did the number of people considered chronically homeless decrease during the three years of the recession, according to the author?
2. According to the author, Dayton, Ohio, was able to save how much per day by moving a group of mentally ill homeless people into housing?
3. According to the author, did overall homelessness in America decrease or increase in 2009?

To see what's happening with the homeless population in America today, consider the following "30s."

In the last three years, during the great recession, the number of people who are considered to be chronically homeless has decreased by 30 percent. Over the same time period, the number of homeless families who are temporarily living in shelters has increased by 30 percent, according to a report last week [mid-June 2010] by the Department of Housing and Urban Development (HUD).

The opposite trends show how far America has come in trying to solve homelessness, and where it needs to redouble its efforts.

The Obama administration is attempting that extra effort with a national plan to eliminate homelessness. The plan, required by Congress, seeks to end chronic and veterans homelessness in five years—10 years for families, youth, and children.

Reducing the Number of Chronically Homeless

Encouragingly, the strategy, titled "Opening Doors," aims to build on the success of the last administration, which concentrated on reducing the numbers of chronically homeless. These are people who are mentally ill or otherwise disabled and who have been without a residence for at least a year, or who have been homeless several times over several years.

The [George W.] Bush administration focused on this group because it is the most expensive and difficult homeless population for cities and counties to care for. Because of their disability, the long-term homeless often shuttle back and forth between shelters, detox centers, hospitals, and jails.

Success in lowering the number of people repeating this debilitating cycle came from a big push by Philip Mangano, who headed the federal Interagency Council on Homelessness under President Bush. Mr. Mangano used federal incentives to get hundreds of communities—local governments, businesses, charities, and religious groups—to work with each other on 10-year plans to actually end chronic homelessness. He stressed solving the problem instead of managing it.

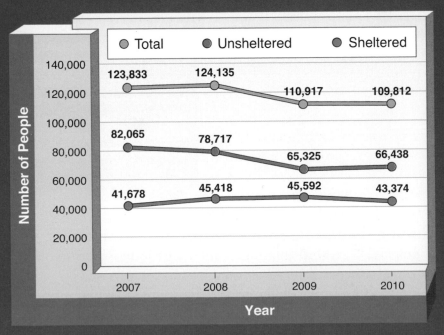

Trends in Chronic Homelessness, 2007–2010

Taken from: Continuum of Care Applications: Exhibit 1, CoC Point-in-Time Homeless Population and Subpopulation, 2007–2010. US Department of Housing and Urban Development. "The 2010 Annual Homeless Assessment Report to Congress," June 14, 2011. www.hud.gov.

A formerly homeless man adjusts the window blinds in an apartment he recently moved into that was made available to him through a "housing-first" program subsidized by state and federal funding.

Mangano furthered an idea dubbed "housing first," a strategy initially funded by Congress in 1999. The concept was elegant in its simplicity. First, help people find stable housing. Once they have the anchor of a residence, support them regularly with caseworkers and social services.

It's a costly, individualized approach, but not nearly as expensive as managing recurring crises. Dayton, Ohio, for instance, found that on the street, one group of mentally ill homeless individuals cost taxpayers $203 a day. Moving them into a 10-unit apartment building and supporting them with health services reduced the cost to $85 a day.

Now, President Obama seeks to extend the housing-first principle to other groups, such as veterans and families. "Stable housing is the foundation upon which people build their lives," the strategy says. Without that, "it is next to impossible to achieve good health, positive educational outcomes, or reach one's economic potential."

It also carries on the collaborative philosophy, in which public and private groups, from job training organizations to health and human services, work with each other. Theoretically, these many players are supposed to keep housing front and center as the starting place for their help—to prevent homelessness, and then to rapidly return people to housing when they lose it.

Theoretically, of course, because coordinating so many players can end up looking like the streets of Washington on a Friday afternoon—gridlock. Or groups may bypass each other entirely and never connect.

At the same time, high unemployment works against an individual's ability to pay for housing, as do high-cost housing markets and the foreclosure rate. So do strapped government budgets—from city hall to the halls of Congress.

And yet, past experience now shows that a housing-first strategy works. Interestingly, overall homelessness in America decreased slightly in 2009, the year of the great recession. According to last week's HUD report, 1.56 million people spent at least one night in a shelter or transitional housing last year—down from 1.6 million in 2008.

It takes time for homelessness to reflect a recession, because people double up or stay with relatives. Even so, the decrease is encouraging, considering the severity of the crisis. And the numbers may actually hold next year [2011], as $1.5 billion in federal economic stimulus money takes hold in the form of rent vouchers and other assistance.

During the Bush administration, advocates for the homeless were clamoring for the federal government to pay more attention to the growing number of families who don't have a permanent place to live. Team Obama appears to have heard that plea. It's far from clear whether they can accomplish their goals—which they acknowledge may be more "aspirational." But wisely, they're building on a proven foundation.

EVALUATING THE AUTHOR'S ARGUMENTS:

In this viewpoint *The Christian Science Monitor* claims that it is important to fight homelessness by giving housing first. Why might someone argue that housing should not be the first problem to address, and what other problem would they argue needs to be addressed first?

Chronically Homeless People Need More than Housing

Melinda Henneberger

"Homeless people . . . need more than a house."

In the following viewpoint Melinda Henneberger argues that proposed solutions to homelessness that only provide temporary housing are not realistic. Henneberger claims that Sacramento's announcement of its plan to end homelessness is suspect because of the challenges of funding and the failure to address issues other than housing. She claims that physical and mental disabilities, along with substance abuse, are challenges faced by many of the chronically homeless and will not be fixed by housing alone. Henneberger is a political writer for the *Washington Post*.

AS YOU READ, CONSIDER THE FOLLOWING QUESTIONS:

1. According to the author, what portion of Sacramento's total homeless population remains unsheltered?
2. The author reports that a Sacramento government official said that economic stimulus money would prevent how many people from becoming homeless?
3. Henneberger claims that what percentage of the Sacramento homeless population suffers from physical or mental disabilities or from substance abuse?

T he good news: Sacramento is ending homelessness! Not so good: They're accomplishing this mission the same way George W. Bush "ended" the war in Iraq, with a media event and balloons.

Last February, *The Oprah Winfrey Show* reported on the shameful tent city of homeless people living along Sacramento's American River. According to the show's initial report, and much of the attention that followed, the encampment's residents included many families who were there as victims of the recession. As it turned out, that wasn't the case. There wasn't a single child in the bunch, and, overwhelmingly, homeless people in the encampment (as elsewhere) had underlying mental-health problems and/or addictions. Still, the part of the story Oprah got right is that in the United States of America, shantytowns disgrace us all. And eventually, the city's mayor, Kevin Johnson, abandoned his view that a properly protected tent city might be part of a temporary solution to an uptick in the number of homeless people. So, what's happened since then? Last month [November 2009], Oprah's reporter returned to see what progress had been made. The city scheduled a coinciding event

FAST FACT

According to the Sacramento County Department of Human Assistance, as of 2011 Sacramento County had 2,358 homeless people, of which 955 remained unsheltered.

that the local newspaper admiringly described as a "pep rally," where crowds cheered the mayor's announcement of a plan to end homelessness in Sacramento. If I thought it might work, I'd be cheering, too.

On November 5, the *Sacramento Bee* reported, "Johnson and other leaders kicked off the 'Sacramento Steps Forward' initiative, with a goal of establishing and fully funding 2,400 housing units for homeless people during the next three years." The event, an editorial noted, "had the feel of a campaign rally, complete with politicians, balloons, flags, and celebrities." Oprah's reporter gushed that she was in awe of how much had been accomplished in such a short time. But beneath all the hoopla is a mere handful of broad and worthy goals, along with hubristic claims about providing "a national model." And according to county statistics, about 1,194 of Sacramento County's official homeless population of 2,800 remain unsheltered. (Last year, those numbers were 1,266 of 2,678; this is progress?)

Homeless Subpopulations in Sacramento County, 2011

	Sheltered*	Unsheltered	Total
Chronically Homeless Individuals	111	242	353
Chronically Homeless Families	0	0	0
Veterans	116	181	297
Severely Mentally Ill	310	309	619
Chronic Substance Abuse	590	377	967
Persons with HIV/AIDS	20	30	50
Victims of Domestic Violence	199	317	516
Unaccompanied Children (under 18)**	7	20	27

*Includes persons in emergency shelters and transitional housing, except chronic homeless individuals and families includes only emergency shelters.

**In 2011, HUD changed the title of this row from "unaccompanied youth" to "unaccompanied children." However, the definition of "any person under age 18 who presented for services alone" remains unchanged.

Taken from: Megan Kurteff Schatz, Phil Alonso, and Katharine Gale. "Sacramento County Homeless Count 2011: Summary Results, Methodology, and Technical Report." MKS Consulting, April 22, 2011.

In the spring, Johnson also hopes to move sixty homeless people into tool sheds—officials are calling them "sleeping cottages"—possibly on an empty lot behind existing emergency shelters. So, to recap, the tent city came down a while ago, and the city now plans to create a . . . hut city? Yes, and according to the *Bee*, even some advocates for the homeless consider this an acceptable "temporary" solution—a "stepping stone," they're calling it. (I only hope this isn't like the "temporary" shed erected at the historical site adjacent to my house; according to town officials, it has been there "temporarily" for twenty-five years.)

As for the 2,400 new units Johnson proposes to build, how will they be financed in a lousy economy when there was no money for them in flush times? When I asked Tim Brown, director of Sacramento Steps Forward, he answered that one-time economic stimulus money from HUD's Homeless Prevention and Rapid Re-Housing Program will be used to help people stay in their homes—and will thus prevent an additional 1,000 people from becoming homeless. None of the stimulus money can be spent on new housing for those already living on the street, though, and Brown could not explain where that funding would come from, given the draconian cuts already underway as a result of California's budget crisis: "I can't say all the funding is in place, but it seems like we'd be able to find it."

There is nothing wrong with aiming high. But I was troubled by Brown's assertion that "at least 70 percent of the homeless population only needs temporary assistance. . . . [They] are getting back on their feet anyway." He is using the narrow government definition of "chronic" homelessness to support the dubious claim that short-term help will suffice for most homeless people. He's also contradicting his own data, which show that at least 75 percent of the local homeless population suffers from significant physical or mental disabilities and/or substance abuse and therefore needs more than temporary help.

It isn't only bureaucrats who, in my view, are fudging the facts. For as long as I have been following this issue as a volunteer and as a reporter, some advocates for people living on the street have been loath to admit there are almost always underlying problems, perhaps out of a desire to shield those they're trying to help from public disapproval. That reluctance to make homeless people "look bad" has only

This "tent city" in Sacramento, California, was the subject of an Oprah Winfrey Show *report. Many of the residents turned out to be mentally handicapped or addicted to drugs and thus in need of more than housing help.*

made it more difficult for them to get the treatment and long-term support they need.

As long as the word "homeless" has existed, so has the tension between those who feel our responsibility is to feed, clothe, and shelter people in need—and those who wonder whether prioritizing emergency needs almost inevitably prevents people from addressing long-term problems. In theory, we all say we should do both—and I disagree with those who use "Jesus doesn't want us to enable addictions" as an excuse to do nothing. Still, at what point does the wrong kind of help actually hurt? It's a complicated moral call for sure, but homeless people do need more than a house—and a lot more than a 150-square-foot tool shed. Maybe we could start by recognizing that part of the problem is our political addiction to unrealistic five-point plans.

EVALUATING THE AUTHOR'S ARGUMENTS:

In this viewpoint Melinda Henneberger argues that homeless people need more than a house. For this reason, do you think she would be in favor of or against a housing-first strategy, as endorsed by *The Christian Science Monitor* in the previous viewpoint?

Viewpoint 3

Government Programs Can and Should Be Used to End Homelessness

"The real issue isn't big or small government, but smart government."

Shaun Donovan

In the following viewpoint Shaun Donovan argues that the federal government's plan to end homelessness is necessary and achievable. Donovan argues that communities around the United States have been showing that government programs can work to end homelessness. He contends that the two strategies that have produced results—permanent supportive housing and homeless prevention through rapid rehousing—should be funded and pursued. Donovan is the US secretary of housing and urban development.

AS YOU READ, CONSIDER THE FOLLOWING QUESTIONS:

1. Donovan claims that three hundred communities committed themselves to ending chronic homelessness and have reduced the chronically homeless by what fraction in five years?
2. The author contends that the number of beds for permanent supportive housing has increased by what percentage since 2007?
3. The author says the Barack Obama administration's plan is to end homelessness among families and children by what year?

Shaun Donovan, "Ending Homelessness in Our Time: Why Smart Government Is Key," *The Public Manager,* vol. 40, no. 4, Winter 2011, pp. 23–27. Copyright © 2011 *The Public Manager and The Bureaucrat.* All rights reserved. Adapted and reproduced by permission of the American Society for Training & Development and The Bureaucrat.

In the current political climate, the debate over government's role has often been about "more versus less"—more government services, programs, and taxpayer dollars, versus reduced services, fewer rules, and less federal investment. But my two decades of experience in the public and private sectors tells me that families sitting around the kitchen table and sending their kids to school every morning aren't interested in abstract theories about whether government should be big or small. They simply want to know whether it can be smart and whether their tax dollars are producing results that impact their lives and communities in a positive way.

Of all the challenges I've faced as President [Barack] Obama's Secretary of Housing and Urban Development (HUD) these past three years [2009, 2010, and 2011], few illustrate this point more clearly than the issue of homelessness. America pays an extraordinary price for homelessness: from the tremendous human toll it takes on the men, women, and especially children caught up in the nightmare existence of life on the streets, to the costs associated with the revolving door of shelters, emergency rooms, and jail cells that result. Perhaps the steepest cost associated with homelessness is the mistaken belief that nothing can be done to stop it.

The Fight Against Chronic Homelessness

Less than a decade ago, it was widely believed that people we often refer to as "chronically homeless"—those who struggle with chemical dependency and mental illness and cycle through the shelter, criminal justice, and healthcare systems—would always be homeless. Some even suggested these people wanted to be homeless.

But leaders outside Washington—from rural Mankato, Minnesota, to urban San Francisco—refused to believe the chronically ill, long-term homeless population couldn't be helped. More than 300 communities committed themselves to ending chronic homelessness, partnering with local and state agencies and the private and nonprofit sectors. By combining housing and supportive services, they led a remarkable fight that has reduced the number of chronically homeless by more than a third in five years.

These communities are proving what just a few years ago seemed nearly impossible: that homelessness can be solved in America. Not reduced or managed, but actually ended.

That is why President Obama's bold commitment to ending homelessness is so important. In releasing *Opening Doors: The Federal Strategic Plan to Prevent and End Homelessness in 2010*, President Obama made clear that ending homelessness is the right thing to do for America's homeless population and the smart thing to do for taxpayers.

The most far-reaching and ambitious plan in our history to put the nation on a path toward ending all types of homelessness, *Opening Doors*, represents the culmination of more than a decade of testing new approaches and implementing new strategies in communities around the country. It commits our country to ending chronic homelessness and homelessness among veterans in five years, and ending homelessness for families, youth, and children within a decade, while putting us on a path to end all homelessness—breaking down bureaucracy and funding what works to get results.

Secretary of housing and urban development (third from left) Shaun Donovan meets with Alaska housing officials about homelessness and low-income housing opportunities. Donovan believes that government programs can end homelessness.

Lessons from Battling Homelessness

Over the past three decades, we've learned a lot about homelessness. The most important lesson is that in almost every case, homelessness isn't an intractable problem, but one that can be solved with the right tools and approaches.

Second, we've learned that one size doesn't fit all: different populations have different needs that sometimes require very different solutions. For instance, where a veteran returning from Afghanistan might need treatment for post-traumatic stress disorder to stay stably housed, the solution to homelessness for a family may be something as simple as paying a security deposit or a utility bill.

At a time when we should be using every taxpayer dollar as effectively and efficiently as possible, we need to focus our resources on doing what works—on evidence-based solutions that have been tried, tested, and have produced results. The two approaches that have shown the most success for the largest number of people are permanent supportive housing and rapid re-housing.

The Success of Permanent Supportive Housing

Over the last five years, and beginning with the [George W.] Bush administration, the emergence of permanent supportive housing—housing connected with health and social services—has literally changed the face of homelessness in many communities. Working in collaboration with the federal government, localities have created thousands of units of permanent supportive housing and reduced the number of chronically homeless people across the nation by more than a third.

The number of beds for permanent supportive housing has increased by 34 percent since 2007. Because affordable housing with necessary services generally costs less than those associated with multiple emergency room visits and stays in jail, this shift in focus to permanent supportive housing has saved significant money for the taxpayer.

Armed with this proven success, HUD, with support from President Obama and Congress, has made an unprecedented commitment to permanent supportive housing to end homelessness for people with severe disabilities and long histories of homelessness.

Homeless Prevention and Rapid Re-housing

Another proven solution to ending homelessness that we've embraced is the combination of prevention and rapid re-housing. In 2009, the American Recovery and Reinvestment Act created the Homeless Prevention and Rapid Re-housing Program (HPRP), and earlier this year [2011], the program marked an important milestone, saving more than 1 million people from homelessness.

HPRP has helped homeless men and women transition into permanent supportive housing—often providing those at risk of homelessness with something as simple as a security deposit. For the majority of the people assisted by HPRP to date, it was the pro-

FAST FACT

In fiscal year 2012 Congress allotted $18.91 billion for Tenant-Based Rental Assistance, including $75 million for new vouchers for homeless veterans.

gram's ability to help them find or stabilize housing arrangements quickly and effectively that made the difference.

Grantees report that fully 90 percent of people assisted by HPRP in its first year successfully found permanent housing. In a state like Michigan, 94 percent of homeless persons in rapid re-housing didn't fall back into homelessness. That's an impressive record.

Examples Around the Country

We've seen similar successes across the country. These funds have helped speed progress in states like Utah, which over the last few years has invested in permanent supportive housing—helping reduce chronic homelessness by nearly 70 percent since 2005. By targeting its HPRP resources to rapid re-housing, Utah was able to reduce chronic homelessness an astounding 26 percent over the last year alone.

In addition, HPRP introduced a new federal commitment to help people avoid homelessness altogether. According to the report, more than three out of every four people assisted by HPRP received homelessness prevention services.

While the lives of those who were homeless or at risk of homelessness have been helped dramatically by the HPRP approach, just as

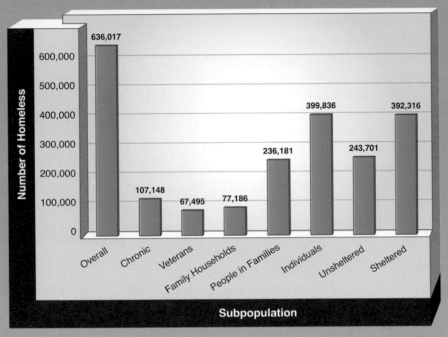

Homeless Population and Subpopulations, 2011

Taken from: National Alliance to End Homelessness and Homeless Research Institute. "The State of Homelessness in America 2012," January 2012. www.naeh.org.

significant is how HPRP is "fundamentally changing" the way communities respond to homelessness, as the U.S. Conference of Mayors put it.

For instance, Cleveland's Continuum of Care program is using HPRP funds to create a central intake system that provides customized services to those entering the shelter system. This helps the community not only manage beds and services more effectively but also ensures that households are transitioning to permanent housing as quickly as possible.

Cleveland provides a good example of how a federal program like HPRP is helping communities move from fragmented, duplicative programs to a comprehensive 21st century system that targets resources to those most in need—not with top-down rules, but with flexible tools from the ground up. . . .

Ending Homelessness in Our Time

As we finish the first year of the Obama administration's effort to end homelessness under the *Opening Doors* strategic plan, there is much work left to be done. But already we are beginning to see results—even in the midst of the most difficult economy in decades—as we work to end homelessness among families and children by 2020, end chronic and veteran homelessness by 2015, and put ourselves on a path to end all types of homelessness.

In this age of budget deficits, some say we can't afford to be that ambitious, but I believe we can't afford not to. Whether it's Utah ending homelessness for 7-in-10 of the hardest-to-house members of the population or HUD-VASH [Veterans Affairs Supportive Housing] beating its goal of housing homeless veterans by nearly 50 percent, these efforts demonstrate that the real issue isn't big or small government, but smart government.

With smart government, we can solve big problems. Few problems are bigger than homelessness. And to be sure, we will have to make our case for resources in not just this budget cycle, but in every one.

By focusing on approaches with proven success, by finding new and better ways to use existing resources, by building partnerships to provide comprehensive solutions, and by holding ourselves accountable for producing results, we can make that case—and we can end homelessness in our time.

Much work remains to be done. But with President Obama in the White House, we not only have a president who believes that no one should experience homelessness, we also have the leadership, tools, and plan in place that we need to see a day in which no one will.

EVALUATING THE AUTHOR'S ARGUMENTS:

In this viewpoint Shaun Donovan rejects criticism of the federal plan to end homelessness based on affordability. How might Donovan justify the cost to individual taxpayers?

Private Charity, Not Government Programs, Should Be Used to End Homelessness

"The answer is not simply more money for more government programs, of which there are thousands nationwide."

Doug Bandow

In the following viewpoint Doug Bandow argues that individuals and private entities, rather than political authorities, can address the needs of the homeless. He claims that homelessness often is a reflection of a personal crisis and that part of the problem is a failure to behave responsibly. When homelessness occurs, Bandow contends that family and friends should be the first to respond, followed by private charities. Government, he argues, often worsens the problem of homelessness through housing regulations and federal involvement in a local problem. Bandow is a senior fellow at the Cato Institute.

Doug Bandow, "Handling America's Homeless Families," *Washington Times,* May 17, 2009, pp. 1–3, 7–8. Copyright © 2009 The Washington Times LLC. This reprint does not constitute or imply any endorsement or sponsorship of any product, service, company or organization. License # 34142

AS YOU READ, CONSIDER THE FOLLOWING QUESTIONS:
1. According to the author, approximately how many homeless people were there as of January 2007?
2. Bandow argues that private social programs are better than government initiatives for what reason?
3. Bandow proposes that what four federal subsidy programs used to encourage homeownership should be reduced?

With the economy in apparent freefall, human needs, including homelessness, have grown. Our starting point should be moral, not political.

During the dramatic biblical parable of the sheep and goats, Jesus asserts our moral responsibility rather than debates our policy approach.

Matthew quotes Jesus as telling the sheep: "For I was hungry and you gave me something to eat, I was thirsty and you gave me something to drink, I was a stranger and you invited me in." They ministered to Jesus by doing these things "for one of the least of these brothers of mine."

This duty cannot be subcontracted to government. The Bible demonstrates concentric rings of responsibility moving outward, starting with individuals who are enjoined to take care of themselves, rather than living off of others. Those who fail to care for their families are worse than unbelievers, Paul warns. The early church transferred money within and among faith communities. Finally, Paul says in Galatians, "let us do good to all people."

If the political authorities are to act, it should be because other institutions have failed to meet people's basic needs. Today, far more private than public programs serve the homeless. The Catholic and Protestant doctrines of subsidiarity and sphere sovereignty, respectively, recognize that government is to respect the roles of other social institutions.

Diversity of responses is particularly important in dealing with a problem as complicated as homelessness. Even the number of homeless is disputed.

The Department of Housing and Urban Development figures homelessness on any particular night (in or out of a shelter) ran

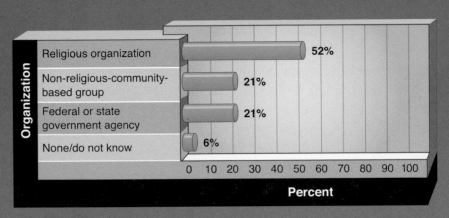

Who can do the best job feeding the homeless?

Organization

	Percent
Religious organization	52%
Non-religious-community-based group	21%
Federal or state government agency	21%
None/do not know	6%

0 10 20 30 40 50 60 70 80 90 100

Percent

Taken from: Pew Research Center for the People & the Press and Pew Forum on Religion & Public Life, 2009 Religion & Public Life Survey," August 2009.

672,000 as of January 2007—down about 10 percent from 2005. There were 84,000 homeless households, down 15 percent. Chronic homelessness ran 124,000, down 30 percent.

The drop is positive, though these numbers remain far too high, and may have turned up in the current economic imbroglio [complicated situation].

The reasons for homelessness run the gamut. Those in poverty long have had difficulty finding affordable housing.

Dubious mortgages, declining home prices and increasing unemployment are threatening many homeowners today. The rising tide of foreclosures puts entire families at risk.

Homelessness also often reflects personal crisis, such as family breakdown, substance abuse and/or mental illness. The deinstitutionalization movement, which sought to respect the dignity of those who had been forcibly medicated and hospitalized, left some people living on the streets. Alcohol or drug use often accentuated other problems.

The answer is not simply more money for more government programs, of which there are thousands nationwide. This enormous challenge can be best met by reflecting back on the biblical model. We need to simultaneously meet current needs, which often include illness and hunger, and reduce future problems.

First, individuals and families have a moral as well as practical imperative to behave responsibly. Americans need to relearn how to resist substance abuse, curb wasteful expenditures and save money. Borrowers and lenders alike should spend money wisely.

Second, family and friends, backed by churches and other social networks, should be the first line of defense to homelessness. The need may be as simple as temporary financial aid or an empty couch. Such informal assistance can soften the impact of unexpected hardship while preserving the dignity of those in need.

Third, private social programs are better than government initiatives in ministering to the whole person, rather than treating those in trouble as numbers and prescribing only a check or bed. Some of the neediest require proverbial "tough love"—compassion and discipline. It is important to keep people off the street and ensure that they won't face the same problem again. That often requires changes in behavior as well as circumstance.

FAST FACT

According to a 2012 study by the *Chronicle of Philanthropy*, Americans on average give 4.7 percent of their income to charity.

Obviously, charities have been affected by the current economic slump. However, this provides an opportunity for advocacy by activists and preaching by religious leaders. Those concerned about the needy must remind all of us of our duty to help, especially in difficult times. To whom much is given, much is expected, the Bible explains.

Fourth, local initiatives are most likely to be effective in meeting needs that vary dramatically by region. Unfortunately, the results of many of the federal welfare programs, including those directed at housing, ranging from rental vouchers to Section 8 to public housing, have been ugly. The government's safety net is best maintained by states and localities rather than by Washington.

Homeless men crowd into a Catholic Charities homeless shelter in Las Vegas, Nevada. Conservatives believe that private charities, not the federal government, are best equipped to help the homeless.

Fifth, the many federal subsidy programs used to encourage homeownership—Federal Housing Administration, Community Reinvestment Act, Fannie Mae, Freddie Mac—are ground zero of today's housing crisis and should be curbed. Attempts to solve the current crisis by artificially reinflating home values risk rewarding improvident lenders and borrowers alike, delaying painful but necessary adjustments in the housing market, and creating conditions for repeat experience in the near future.

We should instead make housing less expensive. Through exclusionary zoning (including restrictions on multifamily housing and minimum-lot size and square-footage requirements) and outmoded building codes (which reflect union interests rather than safety concerns), government has limited the housing supply and increased housing costs. Palliatives like rent control only worsen the underlying problem; government should strip away barriers to affordable housing. Doing so would help reduce homelessness.

Good people in a good society take care of those in need. That includes the homeless. But just as the problem is complex, so is the solution. And we will do best if we respond first at a human rather than at a political level.

EVALUATING THE AUTHOR'S ARGUMENTS:

In this viewpoint Doug Bandow argues that political authorities should only act if other private institutions fail to meet people's basic needs. How would Shaun Donovan, author of the previous viewpoint, respond to this claim?

Government Housing Vouchers Are a Highly Effective Form of Assistance

Center on Budget and Policy Priorities

"Research findings indicate that vouchers are a highly effective form of housing assistance."

In the following viewpoint the Center on Budget and Policy Priorities (CBPP) argues that the federal low-income housing assistance program that provides vouchers to help low-income people pay rent or buy homes is a valuable program that should continue. The CBPP claims that housing vouchers can protect children from homelessness, help families move out of poor neighborhoods, lift families above the poverty line, and promote work. The CBPP is an organization working at the federal and state levels on fiscal policy and public programs that affect low- and moderate-income families and individuals.

AS YOU READ, CONSIDER THE FOLLOWING QUESTIONS:
1. According to the author, how many households does the Housing Choice Voucher Program assist?
2. Under the housing voucher program, according to the author, housing agencies are required to ensure that three-quarters of new recipients have incomes below what percentage of the area median?
3. The author points to a study finding that housing vouchers have the strongest effect on preventing homelessness on families with children under what age?

The Housing Choice Voucher Program (sometimes referred to as the "Section 8 voucher program" after the section of the U.S. Housing Act that authorizes it) is the largest federal low-income housing assistance program. Families who are awarded vouchers use them to help pay the cost of renting housing on the open market. Because most vouchers are provided to particular tenants to live where they choose, they are often referred to as "tenant-based" assistance. Vouchers can also be used to help families buy homes, or [are] tied to particular affordable-housing developments.

The Housing Choice Voucher Program

The voucher program is administered at the federal level by the Department of Housing and Urban Development (HUD). At the local level, the program is run by approximately 2,400 local, state, and regional housing agencies, known collectively as public housing agencies (PHAs). Many of these are independent public authorities, while others are part of city, county, or state governments and thus are directly under the supervision of elected officials. (About 30 housing agencies participate in the Moving-to-Work (MTW) demonstration. MTW, which was authorized by Congress in 1996, permits HUD to enter into temporary agreements with a limited number of housing agencies to waive many of the federal rules governing the voucher and public housing programs.)

The Section 8 program was established in 1974 during the Nixon-Ford Administration. Major changes to the tenant-based portion of the program were made by legislation passed in 1983, 1987, and 1998. As part of the 1998 legislation, Congress merged the two previous components of the tenant-based Section 8 program—certificates and vouchers—into a single housing program.

The voucher program currently assists more than 2 million households. It is the only federal housing program primarily serving poor families that has grown as needs have grown over the last 20 years. The emergence of vouchers as the centerpiece of federal low-income housing policy reflects a major shift during the last 30 years toward more market-based housing subsidies. Previously, the federal government had focused on supporting the construction of public housing or on subsidizing affordable private housing with project-based subsidies.

Housing vouchers are not an entitlement benefit. Because of funding limitations, only one in four households that are eligible for vouchers receive any form of federal housing assistance. Most areas have long and growing waiting lists for vouchers, and a 2004 study found that 40 percent of the housing agencies examined had closed their waiting lists to new applicants because the lists had become so long.

The need for housing assistance is very great. HUD's most recent analysis of Census data indicates that in 2005, 6.5 million low-income renter households that did not receive housing assistance had "severe housing problems," which means they either paid more than half of their income for rent and utilities or lived in severely substandard rental housing. This number increased by 20 percent between 2001 and 2005. High housing-cost burdens contribute to housing instability and homelessness, which in turn have cascading effects on the well-being of children and other family members. Working families are among those who struggle the most to afford housing. A majority of the low-income families without housing assistance who face severe housing problems (excluding those who get Social Security) are working families.

Eligibility for Housing Vouchers

Income eligibility limits for the voucher program are set as percentages of the median income in the local area. (Each year HUD estimates the median income for households of different sizes in every metropolitan area and rural county in the nation.) State and local housing agencies have substantial flexibility to determine which families they

A homeless veteran holds his housing voucher paperwork for permanent housing. The voucher program, many argue, is an effective tool in the fight against homelessness.

will serve, and are permitted to establish admission preferences based on household characteristics (such as preferences for working families or families that live in particular areas) or on housing needs such as homelessness.

Income limits. Each housing agency must set the overall income cap for families admitted to its voucher program between 50 percent and 80 percent of the local area median income. (Nationally for a family of three in 2009, HUD's estimates of 50 percent of median income averaged $31,100, and 80 percent of median income averaged $49,000) Technically, a housing agency may only set the overall income cap above 50 percent of area median income if it states a reason for doing so in its annual plan for the voucher program, but this requirement does little to restrict agencies' flexibility.

Income limits are only applied at the time a family enters the voucher program, so a family can continue to use its voucher if its income later rises above the limit. The amount of a voucher subsidy falls as a family's income rises, however, and in practice a family's subsidy generally fades to zero before (or soon after) its income reaches 80 percent of area median income.

Who Is Helped by Housing Vouchers?

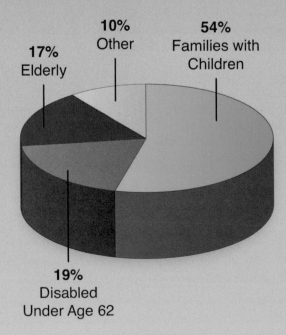

10%
Other

54%
Families with
Children

17%
Elderly

19%
Disabled
Under Age 62

Taken from: CBPP analysis of HUD RCA data for December 1, 2007 through March 31, 2009. Center on Budget and Policy Priorities. "Introduction to the Housing Voucher Program," May 15, 2009. www.cbpp.org.

Targeting to the neediest families. Housing agencies are required to ensure that 75 percent of households newly admitted to the voucher program each year have incomes at or below 30 percent of the area median. (Nationally, 30 percent of median income averaged $18,700 for a family of three in 2009, close to the poverty line.) The targeting requirement is only applied when families are first admitted to the voucher program.

HUD refers to households with incomes up to 80 percent of the area median as *low-income* households, those with incomes up to 50 percent of the area median as *very low-income* households, and those with incomes up to 30 percent of the area median as *extremely low-income* households. . . .

FAST FACT

The amount of rent a housing voucher can cover is capped by a payment standard, which is between 90 and 110 percent of what the US Department of Housing and Urban Development estimates is the fair market rent in the area.

The Effects of Housing Vouchers

Research findings indicate that vouchers are a highly effective form of housing assistance. A 2002 report by the U.S. General Accounting Office found that vouchers are more cost-effective than federal programs that build affordable housing for low-income households. In addition, research shows that housing vouchers promote positive outcomes for families.

Protecting children from homelessness and housing instability. A 2006 study found that families with children who were issued vouchers experienced sharply lower rates of homelessness compared to a control group, with the strongest effect on families with children under age 6. The same study found that vouchers greatly reduced the number of times families moved from apartment to apartment. Both homelessness and housing instability have been linked to a variety of developmental and health problems in children.

Helping families move out of high-poverty neighborhoods. Vouchers have been shown to help families move from areas with high poverty rates to neighborhoods with lower poverty and higher employment.

Researchers have found that using a voucher to move to a low-poverty neighborhood produces a range of positive effects on family well-being, including lower rates of some mental and physical health problems. The effects on mental health—including depression, anxiety, and sleep problems—were particularly striking. By some measures, using a voucher to move to a low-poverty area reduced mental health problems as much as the most effective clinical treatments and medications.

Lifting families above the poverty line. Vouchers substantially reduce the number of families living in poverty (when near-cash income like housing subsidies is taken into account along with cash income), enabling families to spend more on other basic needs. Among the most vulnerable families with children, for example, vouchers have been found to lower the incidence of food insecurity and reduce the number of families that went without dental care because they could not afford it.

Supporting work. Vouchers and other housing assistance play a key role in helping low-income working families make ends meet. Critics have argued that because rents under the voucher program rise as a family's income increases, vouchers may discourage work. But the most rigorous study to date of families with vouchers refuted this theory, finding no significant negative effect on earnings or employment. Moreover, some studies indicate that vouchers and other housing assistance can promote work, particularly when linked to well-designed welfare reform initiatives or other work incentives and employment services.

Based on such findings, the housing voucher program has received longstanding bipartisan support. For example, the [George W.] Bush Administration noted in its fiscal year 2008 budget documents that "based on an assessment of the [voucher] program, this is one of the Department's and the Federal Government's most effective programs" and that the program "has been recognized as a cost-effective means for delivering decent, safe, and sanitary housing to low-income families." The bipartisan, congressionally chartered Millennial Housing Commission strongly endorsed the voucher program in its 2002 report, describing the program as "flexible, cost-effective, and successful in its mission" and calling for a substantial increase in the number of vouchers.

Government Housing Vouchers Promote Dependency and Poverty

Howard Husock

"Housing vouchers have caused many of the same problems as public housing, including long-term government dependency and the concentration of poverty."

In the following viewpoint Howard Husock argues that federal housing subsidies through rental vouchers have encouraged dependence on government and have increased crime and poverty. Husock contends that although housing vouchers are used for private rentals, they do not have any of the benefits of a true free-market solution. Eliminating government intervention in the form of vouchers and housing regulations, Husock concludes, would result in affordable housing that encourages responsible behavior. Husock is vice president for policy research at the Manhattan Institute and author of *The Trillion-Dollar Housing Mistake: The Failure of American Housing Policy.*

AS YOU READ, CONSIDER THE FOLLOWING QUESTIONS:
1. According to Husock, federal tenant-based aid given to 2 million American households in 2009 cost taxpayers how much?
2. The author claims that most recipients of Section 8 housing vouchers also receive which three additional federal benefits?
3. Husock argues that the private, unsubsidized rental market promotes responsible behavior because tenants and potential homeowners have to do what?

Though crime-ridden public housing projects are the most infamous symbol of federal housing policy, much more funding today goes toward rental subsidies for low-income families in private dwellings. About 2 million households receive federal tenant-based aid, at a taxpayer cost of $16 billion in 2009. In addition, about 1.3 million households benefit from project-based aid, which subsidizes rent in particular buildings at a taxpayer cost of $7.5 billion in 2009.

The Rationale for Housing Vouchers

The idea for rental vouchers originated with [President] Lyndon Johnson's Kaiser Commission on Urban Housing. The commission mistakenly believed that private housing markets could not provide the poor with adequate housing, despite the fact that private markets had been steadily improving housing standards for many decades for families at all income levels. Accepting the commission's rationale, the [Richard] Nixon administration proposed what became Section 8 of the Housing and Community Development Act of 1974, which authorized federal rent subsidies for privately owned apartments.

The rationale for vouchers was straightforward: instead of placing an aid recipient in a government-built housing project, the federal government would provide a voucher that subsidized rent in a privately owned building. Liberals embraced Section 8 vouchers because they believed poor families could not afford decent market-rate housing. Conservatives embraced vouchers because it seemed to be a market-based method of steering the private sector toward serving a public policy goal.

Do you favor or oppose a work requirement for welfare recipients?

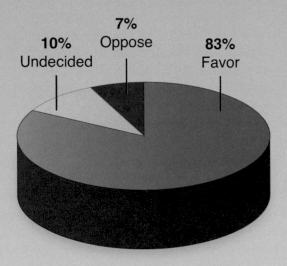

7%
Oppose

10%
Undecided

83%
Favor

Taken from: Rasmussen Reports poll, July 16–17, 2012.

Unfortunately, housing vouchers have caused many of the same problems as public housing, including long-term government dependency and the concentration of poverty. Although traditional federal welfare payments were reformed in 1996 to encourage work and self-sufficiency, Section 8 housing remains an open-ended benefit that recipients can remain on permanently. The problem is compounded by the fact that the value of Section 8 benefits is large. For example, the value of a New York City Housing Authority voucher for a two-bedroom apartment in 2007 was a hefty $1,318.

The Risk of Dependence

Although anyone earning less than 80 percent of the median income initially qualifies for the program, priority for vouchers goes to the poorest applicants. By law, 75 percent of vouchers must go to households earning 30 percent or less of median family income for an area. Local housing authorities can go even further in targeting the poorest applicants, and many do. The result is that vouchers are heavily tilted toward very low income single-parent households.

Today, most Section 8 recipients receive a variety of open-ended federal benefits, including food stamps, Medicaid, and the Earned Income Tax Credit, which together constitute substantial permanent welfare support for single-parent households. These programs and housing vouchers risk encouraging the formation and continuation of government-dependent households. Because Section 8 rent is pegged at 30 percent of income, any increase in a recipient's wages above that amount leads to a steep rent increase, and thus Section 8 creates a strong disincentive for individuals to expand their market earnings and seek personal advancement.

By contrast, unsubsidized housing markets are supportive of a healthy social fabric because they inspire and enable individuals to advance. Private markets reward effort and achievement by giving people the chance to live in better homes in better neighborhoods. As people work hard and gain job experience, they can earn their way to larger homes in nicer neighborhoods. There is no hurdle to improvement, as there is with income-targeted government benefits.

The Creation of Frozen Cities

Whereas public housing projects created highly visible pockets of crime and poverty, Section 8 vouchers were supposed to spread out poor families more widely. But that has not happened, and Section 8 tenants have become concentrated in particular buildings and certain areas of cities. Democratic Senator Barbara Mikulski of Maryland has noted that vouchers have replaced "vertical ghettos with horizontal ones."

Some landlords, in fact, specialize in Section 8, becoming experts at the complex regulations, and they skillfully work the system to their financial advantage. With Section 8 tenants, landlords don't have to worry about nonpayment, because the government deposits its share of the rent—the lion's share—directly into the property owner's bank account. Moreover, for many buildings the government-paid rent is more than the market rent would be. The reason is that the program allows voucher holders to pay up to the average rent in their entire metropolitan area, and landlords in lower-income neighborhoods, where rents are below average, simply charge voucher holders exactly that average rent.

Taken together, both housing vouchers and public housing contribute to the creation of what might be called "frozen cities." Subsidized tenants remain stuck in public housing projects and Section 8 buildings for years, even decades. In addition, the actual buildings that subsidized tenants inhabit remain tied to one particular low-value use, which prevents the affected areas of cities from enjoying the natural changes and upgrading over time that other neighborhoods experience. Neighborhoods with subsidized housing do not get renewed, and they offer fewer opportunities for individuals to improve their lives and their surroundings.

The Issue of the Private Market

Many policymakers remain in thrall of the "free market" voucher. They have yet to grasp that Section 8 vouchers establish no real private market, but are instead merely a categorical income assistance program that has helped to form and perpetuate a social and economic underclass. Republicans have often acquiesced in Section 8 program's growth, while urban Democrats use the program's growing funding to shower benefits on their constituents.

FAST FACT

In 1964 there were 582,000 units of public housing occupied by 2.1 million people, many of which have been demolished in recent decades after becoming dilapidated or crime ridden.

To its credit, the George W. Bush administration tried to freeze funding on traditional Section 8 vouchers, and it pushed for the more than 2,000 local housing authorities across the country to make vouchers less of an open-ended benefit. (To its discredit, however, it also proposed that Section 8 payments be allowed to be used as downpayments on homes!) While Section 8 was originally a Republican program, Democrats have consistently come to the

Seekers of Section 8 housing line up to receive housing vouchers in Bloomington, Indiana. Conservatives say such programs ultimately promote poverty and government dependency.

defense of the program, blocked cuts and reforms, and successfully promoted expansion.

Supporters of subsidized housing have, for more than 70 years, acted on the belief that private markets cannot provide adequate housing for lower-income families. New Deal administrator Harold Ickes frequently made such claims in support of housing subsidies. Ickes claimed that "slums cannot be eradicated except on the basis of a government subsidy." In 1935, Catherine Bauer—an influential public housing crusader at the time—claimed that private housing markets could not serve fully two-thirds of Americans, and thus most people would need public housing assistance. The same year, prominent architect Albert Mayer claimed in a *New York Times* op-ed that 50 percent of the population could not afford to rent in private dwellings. . . .

The Negative Effects of Subsidized Housing

Perversely, subsidized housing advocates usually make matters worse when they try to ban the conditions that offend them. By insisting on unrealistically high regulatory standards that drive up housing prices beyond the means of the poor, they help create housing shortages. Since the New Deal, a flood of regulatory mandates—whether for the number of closets, the square feet of kitchen counter space, or handicapped access—have caused private owners and builders to bypass the low-income market in particular. Under current building codes and zoning laws, much of the distinctive lower-cost housing that shaped the architectural identity of America's cities—such as Brooklyn's attached brownstones with basement apartments—could not be built today.

It is true that even with relaxed building and housing codes, we might not be able to build brand-new housing within the reach of all those with low incomes. But housing structures last for decades, which facilitates the continual passing along of gradually older homes to those of more modest means. When new homes are built for the middle class, their homes are passed along to the lower middle class. When lower-middle-class families move up to better accommodations, they pass their homes and apartments along to those who are poorer, and so it goes.

A major social benefit of private and unsubsidized rental and housing markets is the promotion of responsible behavior. Tenants and potential homeowners must establish a good credit history, save money for security deposits or downpayments, come with good references from employers, and pay the rent or mortgage on time. Renters must maintain their apartments decently and keep an eye on their children to avoid eviction. By contrast, public housing, housing vouchers, and other types of housing subsidies undermine or eliminate these benefits of market-based housing.

Support for housing subsidies rests upon a failure to understand the importance of the means—such as marriage, hard work, and thrift— by which families improve their prospects so they can move to a better home in a better neighborhood. Better neighborhoods are not better because of something in the water but because people have built and sustained them by their efforts, their values, and their commitments. Subsidies are based on the mistaken belief that it is necessary to award a better home to all who claim "need," but it is the effort to achieve the better home, not the home itself, that is the real engine of social improvement.

Chapter 3

How Should Legislation Address Homelessness?

People rally outside the US Capitol in support of legislation designed to end homelessness through expansion of affordable housing and social services for nearly 3.5 million homeless Americans.

Restrictions on Feeding the Homeless Are Discriminatory

"Restrictions on feeding the homeless are unconstitutional, discriminatory, and wrongheaded."

Baylen Linnekin

In the following viewpoint Baylen Linnekin argues that cities around the country are enacting misguided legislation that makes it a crime to feed the homeless and hungry. Linnekin contends that such laws are a bad idea during a time when the need is so great. Furthermore, he claims bans on feeding the homeless in public are unconstitutional not only under the First Amendment's guarantees of freedom of religion and freedom of speech but also under its protection of freedom of assembly. Linnekin is a lawyer and is executive director of Keep Food Legal, a nonprofit organization that advocates in favor of food freedom.

AS YOU READ, CONSIDER THE FOLLOWING QUESTIONS:

1. According to Linnekin, in approximately what year did cities around the country start passing laws that ban feeding the homeless?
2. In what three cities, according to the author, has the American Civil Liberties Union challenged feeding bans?
3. Of all the First Amendment freedoms, which does the author think best protects the rights of people to feed the homeless outdoors in public places?

In 1921, in Boston, an activist named Urbain Ledoux—going by the moniker Mr. Zero—happened on an idea to help unemployed veterans and their families. Ledoux, leader of what he called the "Church of the Unemployed," would "auction" off the veterans in public parks. He hoped that the stark image of such auctions—which brought to mind horrific slave auctions that some still alive at the time would have witnessed in person—would galvanize the public and help find people work.

A Repeat of the Past

In Boston, where one such auction took place on the Common over several days, Ledoux and the veterans were overwhelmed by public support:

> Small sums of cash were given daily; free food was delivered by restaurants and bakeries; an experienced cobbler set up shop to repair the shoes of the jobless; several women volunteered to sew and clean the bed linens; furniture was donated; a local dentist announced that he would take care of any toothaches that occurred among the unemployed; and . . . scores, perhaps hundreds, of Ledoux's followers obtained jobs as a result of the auctions.

Ledoux and his supporters met a different fate in New York City—at least initially. City police refused to let Ledoux's group serve food. When his supporters served food in Bryant Park, police moved in and beat "forty jobless men who had gathered about six elderly women distributing sandwiches, cakes and crullers in the park." The American Civil Liberties Union [ACLU] launched a complaint.

And, though Ledoux stepped into the spotlight from time to time, this was largely the end of his auctioneering days.

Ninety years later, however, the issues raised by Ledoux are again making headlines and prompting litigation, even if the tactics of volunteers, police, and regulators may be a bit less stark.

A Rise in Feeding Bans

Starting in about 2006, several cities began arresting, fining, and otherwise oppressing private individuals and nonprofits that feed the

In 1921 homeless activist Urbain J. Ledoux, aka Mr. Zero, led the "Church of the Unemployed" and auctioned off homeless veterans in a slave market atmosphere in an effort to raise public awareness of the plight of the homeless.

homeless and less fortunate. A 2006 NPR [National Public Radio] report referred to a Las Vegas ban on feeding the homeless—a ban challenged by the Nevada state ACLU chapter—as "among the first of its kind in the country."

The suit went on for four years. As the Nevada ACLU recounted in announcing a pending settlement between the group and the city in 2010:

> The City began ticketing good Samaritans who shared food with more than 24 people, under the belief that giving food to people already in the public park violated statutes requiring permits for gatherings of 25 or more people. When the ACLU of Nevada took issue with this interpretation of permit laws, the City took a more direct approach: it explicitly outlawed the sharing of food with anyone who looked poor.

Terms of the Las Vegas settlement require that police may no longer ban and ticket those feeding or being fed "unless there is evidence of unlawful activity, and in those cases a valid arrest must be made or a citation issued." Which is as it should be.

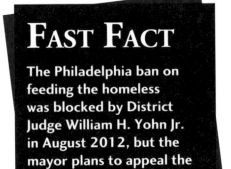

FAST FACT

The Philadelphia ban on feeding the homeless was blocked by District Judge William H. Yohn Jr. in August 2012, but the mayor plans to appeal the decision.

Still, in spite of the suit and settlement, feeding bans like the one initiated in Las Vegas appear to be growing in number around the country.

I blogged at *Hit & Run* last summer [2011] about a ban in Orlando—the first of the most recent spate of such big-city laws. In that case, members of the anti-war group Food Not Bombs had been arrested for feeding the homeless in Orlando city parks.

Since then, other cities have followed suit. In New York City, for example, Mayor Michael Bloomberg banned food donations to the homeless earlier this year [2012] "because the city can't assess their salt, fat and fiber content." Those familiar with Mayor Bloomberg are likely only surprised here that Hizzoner [a contraction of "His Honor"] missed adding sugar to the list of terribles.

A Bad Idea

In a March 2011 piece on a proposed ban on feeding the homeless in Houston, *Take Part* writer Clare Leschin-Hoar noted that the city's ban would have added a panoply of requirements for feeding the homeless there, including limiting food service to three city parks and forcing groups to "register with the city; complete food handlers training courses; prepare food in licensed kitchens; and require a cleanup plan following food service." The ordinance ultimately passed by Houston is a slightly less onerous (though still terrible) one that simply "requires permission from the city government before serving food in city parks."

As it was in Mr. Zero's day, choosing to crack down on those who volunteer to feed the homeless is a bad idea. It's an even worse idea to seize on at a time when lots of people are hungry, food pantries are stretched beyond the breaking point, and increasing numbers of Americans are subsisting on food stamps.

Thankfully, the latest ban to take effect—Philadelphia's, which the aptly named Mayor Michael Nutter implemented just last week [June 1, 2012]—has drawn a legal challenge.

As the Nevada ACLU did in Las Vegas—and the national ACLU did in New York City in the case of the police beating of Ledoux's supporters—the Pennsylvania ACLU chapter finds itself challenging "burdensome restrictions on outdoor feeding programs."

While Mayor Nutter claims the purpose of the ban is to push all "homeless feedings indoors where it is supposedly safer," the state

ACLU counters that the ban was put in place "not to protect the health of the homeless but instead to protect the city's image in a tourist area."

The Constitutional Issues

The suit claims the ban violates the Free Exercise and Free Speech Clauses of the First Amendment and Pennsylvania's Religious Freedom Protection Act. While no doubt true, to those claims I would add that the ban violates the Freedom of Assembly, a First Amendment right that my own research has demonstrated is inextricably intertwined with the provision of food and drink.

A religious group may have separate First Amendment rights to feed the homeless as part of its protected religious mission, just as a group like Food Not Bombs may have separate free-speech rights if feeding the homeless is part of a larger "bake sales versus bombers" protest. But every American enjoys assembly rights separate and distinct from any religious or speech rights—something the Pennsylvania ACLU should make clear here. After all, the U.S. Constitution guarantees the right to assemble peaceably for any reason, while the Pennsylvania Declaration of Rights guarantees that "citizens have a right in a peaceable manner to assemble together for their common good."

Restrictions on feeding the homeless are unconstitutional, discriminatory, and wrongheaded. Courts should force cities to acknowledge that members of civil society have a right to help those in need, and that those in need have a right to obtain assistance outside of government channels.

EVALUATING THE AUTHOR'S ARGUMENTS:

In this viewpoint Baylen Linnekin dismisses the idea that laws banning outdoor feeding of the homeless are justified by safety concerns. Should someone who advocates for the homeless be concerned about the safety of food or only concerned that the homeless get food? Explain.

Restrictions on Feeding the Homeless Are Necessary for Public Safety

"Ensuring minimal food safety standards and working to coordinate food availability is the least we can do for the homeless."

Stephen Williams, Rudy Rasmus, Hank Rush, and Bob Eury

In the following viewpoint Stephen Williams, Rudy Rasmus, Hank Rush, and Bob Eury argue that registration, organization, and coordination of homeless feeding is necessary to ensure food safety and to ensure efficient and effective feeding of those in need. Williams is director of the Houston Department of Health and Human Services and chair of the Coalition for the Homeless of Houston/Harris County, Rasmus is pastor of St. John's Downtown in Houston, Rush is president and chief executive officer of Star of Hope Mission, and Eury is executive director of the Downtown District of Houston.

There are many reasons for homelessness. For some, life on the street is a temporary phenomenon of a struggling economy; for others, it is due to drug abuse or untreated mental illness. Whatever the reason for being there, all homeless people are likely without the means to provide meals for themselves.

A Lack of Coordination

There are 38 known groups and organizations that provide food service to the homeless or others in need of a free meal [in Houston]. Some of

The Salvation Army maintains licensed kitchens and trained staff to comply with local governments' health and safety standards in order to be able to feed the homeless and poor on a regular schedule. Though restrictive, such standards, many argue, are necessary for the greater good.

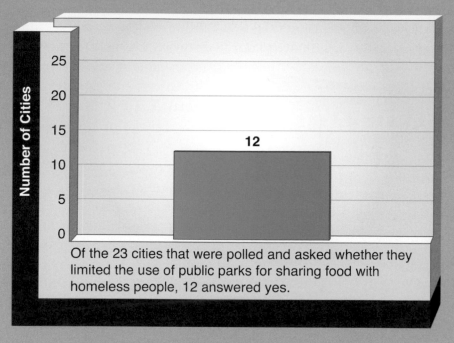

Cities that Limit the Use of Public Parks for Feeding Homeless

Number of Cities

25
20
15
12
10
5
0

Of the 23 cities that were polled and asked whether they limited the use of public parks for sharing food with homeless people, 12 answered yes.

Taken from: The National Coalition for the Homeless and The National Law Center on Homelessness & Poverty. "A Place at the Table: Prohibitions on Sharing Food with People Experiencing Homelessness," July 2010.

these organizations, like the Star of Hope, Palmer Way Station, Bread of Life and the Salvation Army, feed inside their facilities. They have licensed kitchens, trained volunteer staff, are in compliance with the city of Houston's health and safety standards and feed the hungry on a routine schedule.

Unfortunately, there are many other street feeders that do not adhere to routine schedules. For example, there is one location at which a dozen different charitable organizations line up every Saturday morning, all seeking to provide breakfast to the same group of people. There is more than needed for the homeless who show up. In the end, a lot of it winds up left behind on the ground—creating a nuisance for nearby property owners.

There is also concern about ensuring charitable feeding operations abide by minimum health standards. This helps reduce sickness that can create additional public health concerns that can burden our public health care providers.

The Need for a New Ordinance

It is clear there is sufficient food available for the homeless and hungry. What is lacking is sufficient coordination of the food to make sure it is available every day in more locations and to ensure private property is not abused. The solution is registration and coordination of the various charitable feeding operations—a way to require permission to use private property, ensure adherence to minimal health standards and to help the organizations better determine the locations and days that their efforts would be most beneficial. These are the reasons for a new ordinance under consideration by Houston City Council.

FAST FACT

In April 2012 the Houston City Council adopted an ordinance requiring permission to feed the homeless, which went into effect July 1, 2012.

This new ordinance will require organizations and individuals wishing to provide food for the homeless or indigent to:

- Register with the Houston Health Department. There is no charge for this registration and it is valid indefinitely or until the organization ceases operations.
- Complete a food-handlers training course provided at no charge by the health department. The training will include safe food handling procedures, ordinance requirements, strategies for working with the homeless and information and referral for health and social services.
- Obtain written permission from the owner/manager of public or private property at which food will be served.
- Prepare/assemble food in a licensed kitchen (which are readily available throughout the community).
- Require a plan for clean up of trash following food service.

Coordination of the various feeding operations will be handled by the Coalition for the Homeless and the Houston Food Bank, which

© *"Tramp enjoys good food." cartoon by Tony Neat. www.cartoonstock.com.*

will serve as a point [of] entry for new organizations wanting to help or for individuals wanting to work with an established operation.

The Benefits of the Proposal

Registration and coordination of street feeding operations is not a new concept. Ten of the largest U.S. cities already require it, and nine of these cities also require routine inspection for adherence to public health standards.

We seek not to regulate, but to organize and coordinate, street feeding. What is being proposed will not inhibit the many acts of charity conducted daily by Houstonians. In fact, this more efficient and effective food delivery system may well renew interest in helping the homeless, while at the same time protecting private-property rights.

We do not have two standards of food safety in our city; what is good for those who have is also good for those who have not. Ensuring minimal food safety standards and working to coordinate food availability is the least we can do for the homeless.

EVALUATING THE AUTHORS' ARGUMENTS:

In this viewpoint Stephen Williams, Rudy Rasmus, Hank Rush, and Bob Eury claim that the ordinance they propose would not inhibit acts of charity. Based on the requirements of the ordinance, name at least one way that the ordinance could inhibit feeding of the homeless.

Viewpoint

3

"The new federal bill rightly acknowledges that homeless people . . . deserve to be protected from the cruel and brutal treatment of the bigots among us."

The Homeless Need New Legislation to Protect Them from Hate Crimes

Brian Levin and Jack Levin

In the following viewpoint Brian Levin and Jack Levin argue that just like other groups are protected from prejudice, the homeless need legislation to help protect them from bias crime, which has escalated in recent years. Brian Levin is a professor of criminal justice and director of the Center for the Study of Hate & Extremism at California State University, San Bernardino. Jack Levin is the Brudnick Professor of Sociology and Criminology at Northeastern University in Boston, where he codirects its Center on Violence and Conflict, and is coauthor of *The Violence of Hate*.

AS YOU READ, CONSIDER THE FOLLOWING QUESTIONS:
1. According to the authors, what percentage of those attacking the homeless in the past ten years are teenagers?
2. More than what percentage of the homeless are under age five, according to the authors?
3. According to the authors, how many homeless people were murdered between 2005 and 2008?

Hate crime legislation is aimed at protecting the most defenseless among us who are targeted out of prejudice—minority families who relocate to a previously all-white neighborhood where they are met with a burning cross and a threatening phone call rather than the welcome wagon; gay college students who are assaulted by their schoolmates because they are different; the first Latino employee in an office who is warned to leave the company before it is too late.

Hate Crimes Against Homeless People

Clearly, of all those who are targeted for prejudice, homeless members of society are among the most vulnerable of all. They are literally hunted down by everyone from violent racist skinheads to groups of bored and idle teenagers and young adults who get a sadistic thrill out of beating, burning or drowning to death helpless street people. In our highly competitive and increasingly coarse society, negative stereotypes about difference, appearance, and the worth of the poor label the homeless as disposable people. Class based prejudice, which sometimes overlaps with racial hatred among others, remains one of the last widely acceptable forms of intolerance. Yet, homelessness continues to be excluded from most hate crime legislation at the state and federal level. While about a dozen states including California and New York, have considered such measures, only Maryland, Maine and the District of Columbia have added homeless status to their hate crime laws.

Just like teenagers who target Blacks, Muslims, or Latinos, those youngsters out for a thrill who attack homeless people get little more than bragging rights with their friends who think that violence is pretty cool. Their shared violence becomes a bonding ritual, not unlike attacks by gangs or the hazing rituals in some fraternities. The sadism in their crimes may originate in the thinking of one or two cruel but influential members of the group The others are "fellow travelers" who really go along to get along. The last thing they want is to be rejected by their friends.

In order to reminisce about the cherished moments they share causing pain and suffering on the streets, youthful perpetrators have actually been known to videotape their tortures—spurred on by the advent of small cheap video cameras, social Internet media and a series of horrendous commercial "bumfights" videos. In the background, through the horrific screams of their victims, the perpetrators can be heard laughing uncontrollably. In their minds, homeless people deserve their fate; they are viewed as nothing more than garbage or

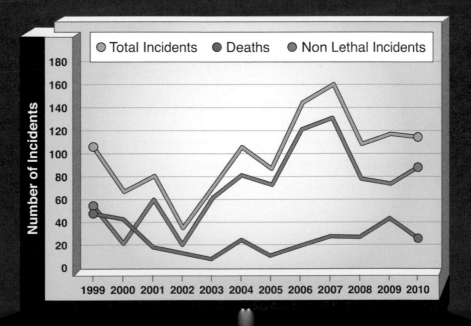

Hate Crimes Against Homeless
Individuals: 1999–2010

Neo-Nazis in Los Angeles attack a homeless man during a street rally. Such incidents have occurred all over the country and have spawned legislation to protect the homeless from hate crimes.

trash to be eliminated from the streets. As with other hate crime offenders, these attackers are typically young male "thrill offenders" seeking excitement and peer validation. Fifty-eight percent of those attacking the homeless over the past 10 years are in the 13–19 age group. These thrill offenders, like the more hardened racist skinhead perpetrators, view attacking the homeless as nothing more than a fun communal way of simply cleaning the streets of filth, an activity to be respected rather than reviled.

An Acceptable Form of Prejudice

Sadly, those young people who attack the homeless reflect a more general prejudice. Homeless people are generally regarded as the dregs of society—as chronically filthy, lazy, passed-out drunk, alone, psychotic, and worthless. They are typically seen as bums who refuse to take a job, beg for money and act violently. Youths pick up and act on a combination of messages sent to them by adults. Whether it be in sporting events, reality television, movies or politics coarse, outrageously dangerous, and even violent behavior is portrayed as funny, cool, and strategically smart. Several months ago *Maxim*, a youth-oriented magazine targeted at college-aged males, mocked the National Hobo Convention in Britt, Iowa, in a blurb titled "Hunt the Homeless." The journal directed its readers to "Kill one for fun. We're 87 percent sure it's legal."

Even Americans who express some sympathy for the homeless tend to accept the stereotype that all of them are motivated by drug and alcohol abuse as well as serious mental illness rather than by such factors as job loss or conflict at home as well. Many Americans also stereotype the homeless as single, working-age men who live, for long periods of time, on the sidewalks, under bridges, on park benches, and in shelters. Actually, more than 40% of the homeless consist of children under the age of five. Moreover, more than two-thirds of homeless teenagers only stay on the streets long enough to resolve their family conflicts and go home. Homeless people come from all walks of life. With the unemployment rate at an exceptionally high 10% nationally, the economic situations of both professional and working-class families can quickly deteriorate into a vicious cycle of job loss, financial problems, health issues, and enormous debt. For some, living on the streets or in a shelter may be their only recourse.

FAST FACT

The Hate Crimes Against the Homeless Statistics Act of 2009 was never passed, but the similar Hate Crimes Against the Homeless Statistics Act of 2011 was referred to committee in December 2011.

In the 1980s and 1990s, Americans discovered hate crimes committed because of a victim's race or religious identity. More recently, we discovered hate crimes based on a victim's sexual orientation, gender, gender identity and disability status. In 2009–2010, it is about time that we turn our attention to the plight of homeless people who are being attacked in growing numbers, based simply on an ugly stereotype. As both Christmas, New Years and the longest night of the season approach it is time that all people of good will turn their compassion for the less fortunate into action. This week across the nation vigils are being held on December 21 [2009] to remember the homeless, while many others will turn their Christmas Day into a day not only of prayer, but of selfless service to the less fortunate.

The Need for Legislation

We can also support legislation known as the Hate Crimes Against the Homeless Statistics Act (S. 1765) which has been placed on the Senate Judiciary Committee schedule this month. If passed, the bill would amend the Hate Crime Statistics Act which already takes note of offenses based on race, religion, national origin, sexual orientation, gender, gender identity and disability status to include hate crimes against the homeless in the data collected by the Attorney General.

If they were included in the annual hate crime inventory taken by the FBI, such offenses might actually be more numerous than other hate attacks. Over the last few years, as increasing numbers of Americans have been forced to live on the streets, by some estimates over one million, there has been a sickeningly high number of sadistic acts of violence directed at the homeless that are not the result of robbery, personal animus or drugs. According to the National Coalition for the Homeless (NCH), fatal attacks on homeless people rose 65% between 2005 and 2008, reaching a total of 70 murders over this four-year period, the number killed has not dipped below 20 a year since 2005.

According to the NCH and the Center for the Study of Hate & Extremism, despite their relatively small numbers, nearly 2 1/2 times more homeless people in America have been killed over the past 10 years in apparent unprovoked bias homicides than the total for all the other hate-crime homicides—on the basis of race, religion, national origin, disability and sexual orientation—combined. The FBI documented just 16 hate-crime homicides nationally for the two most recently available years combined, while the NCH enumerated more than three times as many "hate homicides" against the homeless during the same period.

The passage of the Hate Crimes Against the Homeless Statistics Act, introduced by U.S. Senator Benjamin Cardin, will not mandate financial support to government responses to hate crimes against the homeless. The current legislation would merely require that such hate crimes be reported in addition to other bases for bias motivation. Yet, the current bill is nevertheless important because it provides vital information to those who assist the homeless about how we can better protect them and respond to the brutalization of them. Support for inclusion of the homeless in hate crime legislation ranges from conservative Christian Republicans like Maryland State Senator Alex Mooney to Democrats like California State Senate leader Darrel Steinberg. The new federal bill rightly acknowledges that homeless people—no less than racial and religious groups—deserve to be protected from the cruel and brutal treatment of the bigots among us.

EVALUATING THE AUTHORS' ARGUMENTS:

In this viewpoint Brian Levin and Jack Levin claim that hate crime legislation will simply require that hate crimes against the homeless be reported. Do you think the legislation should go further by punishing hate crimes—crimes motivated by bias—more severely? Why or why not?

The Homeless Do Not Need New Legislation to Protect Them from Hate Crimes

"The amount of crimes committed against the homeless by domiciled individuals . . . does not rise to the level of requiring the federal government to collect statistics on this issue."

David Muhlhausen

In the following viewpoint David Muhlhausen argues that the rate of crimes perpetrated against the homeless does not warrant new hate crime legislation. Muhlhausen claims that the number of homeless people murdered each year is not exceptionally large and that the murder rate of homeless people is barely larger than that for the general public. Furthermore, Muhlhausen claims that homeless people themselves commit a high amount of crime. Muhlhausen is a research fellow in empirical policy analysis at the Heritage Foundation.

David Muhlhausen, "Crime Against the Homeless: Tragic, but a Problem Not Requiring Federal Action," Testimony Before the Subcommittee on Crime and Drugs of the Committee on the Judiciary, United States Senate, September 29, 2010.

AS YOU READ, CONSIDER THE FOLLOWING QUESTIONS:
  1. The author claims that in 2009, murders of homeless people constituted what percentage of all murders?
  2. What was the national murder rate in 2009, according to Muhlhausen?
  3. The author claims that a survey of homeless youth in Los Angeles found that what percentage admitted to having attacked another person with a knife?

A ccording to a National Coalition for the Homeless (NCH) report, *Hate Crimes Against The Homeless: America's Growing Tide of Violence* (hereinafter referred to as the NCH report), asserts that "This year's [2010] report has the horrifying distinction of being the deadliest in a decade, at forty-three reported homicides." While every case of a violent act committed against an innocent homeless person is tragic and should be prosecuted to the fullest extent of the law, the prevalence of these crimes do not rise to a level that requires formal data collection by federal, state, and local governments.

A Questionable Report

Policymakers should be skeptical of the conclusions presented in the NCH report. First, the NCH report uses a highly questionable methodology for estimating crimes against the homeless. Using a variety of sources, the cases of violence against the homeless identified in the NCH report appear to be primarily collected from media reports and homeless advocates. Media coverage is not necessarily a good or accurate measure of any social problem.

Second, the NCH report fails to acknowledge the amount of crime committed by the homeless. The NCH report only focuses on crimes committed by "housed" or domiciled individuals against homeless individuals, while it excludes crimes committed by the homeless against other homeless individuals. More importantly, the report ignores the amount of crime committed by the homeless against domiciled individuals.

Third, and most important, the analysis presented in the NCH report fails to make the case that the federal government should collect

Homeless and National Murder Rate, 2009

	Homeless	Nation
Population	643,067	307,006,550
Murders	43	15,241
Murders Per 100,000	6.7	5.0

Taken from: FBI, Uniform Crime Reports, 2009; National Coalition for the Homeless, *Hate Crimes Against the Homeless: America's Growing Tide of Violence*, August 2010; and US Department of Housing and Urban Development, Office of Community Planning and Development, *The 2009 Annual Homeless Report*, (Washington, DC, June 2010). David Muhlhausen, testimony before the Subcommittee on Crime and Drugs of the Committee on the Judiciary, US Senate, September 29, 2010.

data on crimes against the homeless. The NCH report only counts murders of homeless individuals committed by domiciled persons. This leads one to naturally ask, "How many innocent domiciled and homeless individuals were murdered by the homeless?"

The Number of Homeless Murdered

Over the course of 11 years, the NCH report counts 288 homeless murders with an average of less than 26.2 incidents per year. From 1999 to 2003 . . . the number of homeless murders counted by NCH fell from 49 to 8. From 2003 to 2009, the trend reversed. During this period, the number of homeless murders counted by NCH increased from 8 incidents to 43 incidents. While the highest number of homeless murders was recorded in 1999, NCH notes the number of homeless murders in 2009 is "[m]ost disturbing."

The presentation of the number of homeless deaths in the NCH report does not display the number of homeless murders relative to the total number of all murders recorded in the nation. . . . In 2009, the FBI counted 15,241murders in the United States. . . .

NCH homeless homicides from 1999 to 2009 never accounted [for] more than 0.32 percent of total murders. In 2009, homeless murders were 0.28 percent of all murders. Conversely, all other murders accounted for 99.72 percent in 2009. . . .

While tragic, the minuscule number of homeless murders counted by NCH fails to rise to the level of a national problem that requires federal data collection. Homicides of young black males are a much more pressing problem facing our nation. In 2009, the FBI identified 639 black males under 18 years old were murdered in 2009.

The Rate of Murder

However, when comparing incidents of crime over time or across jurisdictions, the standard practice is to express incidents of crime as a rate. Thus, the NCH count of homeless murders is expressed as the rate of incidents per 100,000 residents. . . . The U.S. Department of Housing and Urban Development estimated that there were 643,067 homeless individuals during a single point-in-time in 2009. The entire population of the United States was over 307 million residents in 2009. Based on these population figures, the rate of homeless individuals murdered by domiciled individuals can be calculated.

The national murder rate of the homeless using the data provided by NCH translates into 6.7 incidents per 100,000 homeless persons in 2009. The national murder rate for the entire national population was 5.0 incidents per 100,000 residents. While the homeless murder rate is higher than the national rate, the difference is neither startling nor a justification for the federal government to begin formally collecting statistics on homeless murders. . . .

> **FAST FACT**
>
> The Federal Bureau of Investigation defines hate crime as "a criminal offense committed against a person, property, or society that is motivated, in whole or in part, by the offender's bias against a race, religion, disability, sexual orientation, or ethnicity/national origin."

While the homeless are frequently victims of crime, the NCH report conveniently failed to address the prevalence of crime committed by the homeless. According to social science research, the homeless are generally not a collection of law abiding individuals.

A survey of 432 homeless youth between the ages of 13 and 23 years of age living in the Hollywood area of Los Angeles found that

This citizens' memorial is for a homeless man who was murdered on the streets of Los Angeles in January 2012. Conservatives believe that because murders of the homeless only account for 0.32 percent of all murders there is no need for special legislation to protect the homeless.

25 percent admitted to having attacked another person with a knife (17 percent since residing on the streets) and 22 percent reported having fired a gun at someone (14 percent since residing on the streets). Another study of 200 homeless youth residing in Edmonton, Alberta, Canada, found that they reported, on average, committing 3.11 property crimes, 2.89 drug deals, and 0.87 robberies over an undisclosed period of time. . . .

The Need for Legislation

When Congress considers the need for collecting data on any social phenomena, the nature of the evidence presented to Congress should be instrumental to the decision-making process. A wrong assessment of the evidence can lead Congress to waste valuable resources of the federal, state, and local governments. The NCH draws conclusions far beyond the data presented in its report. An objective and fair analysis of the data presented in the NCH report simply does not support the notion that the federal government needs to collect statistics on crimes committed against the homeless by domiciled individuals.

The amount of crimes committed against the homeless by domiciled individuals, let alone such incidents motivated by "hate," does not rise to the level of requiring the federal government to collect statistics on this issue. Crimes against the homeless, like all other ordinary street crimes, should be prosecuted to the fullest extent of the law by state and local governments.

While some may argue that the lack of reliable data on the number of crimes committed against the homeless by domiciled individuals is justification enough for federal intervention, such logic leads the federal, state, and local governments down the road of collecting data on any perceived social problem, whether the problem warrants attention or not. The Hate Crimes Against the Homeless Statistics Act of 2009 is unnecessary.

EVALUATING THE AUTHOR'S ARGUMENTS:

In this viewpoint David Muhlhausen claims that homeless people commit a disproportionate amount of crime. How does this factor into his argument against hate crime legislation?

Facts About Homelessness

Editor's note: These facts can be used in reports to add credibility when making important points or claims.

Homelessness in America

According to the US Interagency Council on Homelessness, homelessness takes three forms:

- Unsheltered homeless are living on the streets, camping outdoors, living in cars, or living in abandoned buildings.
- Sheltered homeless are staying in emergency shelters or transitional housing.
- Doubled-up homeless are temporarily staying with family or friends.

According to the US Department of Housing and Urban Development, in 2011:

- On any single night, 636,017 people in America were homeless.
- Approximately 17 percent of the homeless, 107,148 people, were chronically homeless.
- Approximately 40 percent of the homeless, 243,701 people, were unsheltered.
- Approximately 10 percent of the homeless, 67,495 people, were veterans.

Risk Factors for Homelessness

According to the US Department of Housing and Urban Development:

- The odds of experiencing homelessness are 1 in 194 for the general population.
- The odds for people with incomes at or below the federal poverty line are one in twenty-nine.
- The odds for veterans are one in ten.

According to the US Department of Justice's Bureau of Justice Statistics:

- The odds of experiencing homelessness for a person discharged from prison or jail are estimated to be one in thirteen.

According to the US Department of Health and Human Services:

- The odds of experiencing homelessness for a youth emancipated from foster care are estimated to be one in eleven.

Poverty and Housing Costs

According to the US Census Bureau's 2010 American Community Survey:

- Housing is considered affordable when it accounts for 30 percent or less of monthly household income.
- Twenty-five percent of US renter households spend 50 percent or more of their monthly income for housing.
- Seventy-five percent of households at or below the poverty line spend 50 percent or more of their monthly income for housing.
- In 2010 there were more than 2.8 million foreclosures on residential units, in which owners lost their homes.

Legislation Affecting the Homeless

A 2009 report by the National Coalition for the Homeless surveyed 235 cities for legislation affecting the homeless and found:

- Thirty-three percent prohibit camping in particular public places in the city, and 17 percent have citywide prohibitions on camping.
- Thirty percent prohibit sitting or lying down in certain public places.
- Forty-seven percent prohibit loitering in particular public areas, and 19 percent prohibit loitering citywide.
- Forty-seven percent prohibit begging in particular public places, 49 percent prohibit aggressive panhandling, and 23 percent have citywide prohibitions on begging.

Organizations to Contact

The editors have compiled the following list of organizations concerned with the issues debated in this book. The descriptions are derived from materials provided by the organizations. All have publications or information available for interested readers. The list was compiled on the date of publication of the present volume; the information provided here may change. Be aware that many organizations take several weeks or longer to respond to inquiries, so allow as much time as possible for the receipt of requested materials.

Canadian Alliance to End Homelessness (CAEH)
925 Seventh Ave. SW, Ste. 308
Calgary, AB T2P 1A5
(403) 718-8526
website: www.caeh.ca

The CAEH aims to create a national movement to end homelessness in Canada. The alliance works to raise awareness of homelessness, provide communities with information and tools to end homelessness, and change provincial and federal policy to support ending homelessness. Among the CAEH's publications is *A Plan, Not a Dream: How to End Homelessness in 10 Years*, available at its website.

Cato Institute
1000 Massachusetts Ave. NW
Washington, DC 20001-5403
(202) 842-0200
fax: (202) 842-3490
website: www.cato.org

The Cato Institute is a public policy research foundation dedicated to limiting the role of government, protecting individual liberties, and promoting free markets. The Cato Institute commissions a variety of publications, including books, monographs, briefing papers, and other studies. Among its publications are the quarterly magazine *Regulation*, the bimonthly *Cato Policy Report*, and articles such as "Homeless Scare Numbers."

Center for Law and Social Policy (CLASP)
1200 Eighteenth St. NW, Ste. 200
Washington, DC 20036
(202) 906-8000
fax: (202) 842-2885
e-mail: info@clasp.org
website: www.clasp.org

CLASP is a national nonprofit organization that seeks to improve the lives of low-income people. Through research, analysis, and advocacy, CLASP develops and promotes new ideas, mobilizes others, and directly assists governments and advocates for the homeless to put in place successful strategies. CLASP publishes many reports, briefs, and fact sheets, including *Families on the Edge: Young Homeless Parents and Their Welfare Experiences*.

Center on Budget and Policy Priorities (CBPP)
820 First St. NE, Ste. 510
Washington, DC 20002
(202) 408-1080
fax: (202) 408-1056
e-mail: center@cbpp.org
website: www.cbpp.org

The CBPP is a policy organization working at the federal and state levels on fiscal policy and public programs that affect low- and moderate-income families and individuals. The center conducts research and analysis to help shape public debates over proposed budget and tax policies and to help ensure that policy makers consider the needs of low-income families and individuals in these debates. Among the CBPP's publications are a series of brief background reports, *Policy Basics*, among which is the recent *Housing Choice Voucher Program*.

Children's Defense Fund (CDF)
25 E St. NW
Washington, DC 20001
(800) 233-1200
e-mail: cdfinfo@childrensdefense.org
website: www.childrensdefense.org

The CDF is a nonprofit child advocacy organization that works to ensure a level playing field for all children. The CDF champions policies and programs that lift children out of poverty; protect them from abuse and neglect; and ensure their access to health care, quality education, and a moral and spiritual foundation. The organization publishes a variety of reports and other documents, including "Black and White: Black Children Compared to White Children."

Coalition on Human Needs
1120 Connecticut Ave. NW, Ste. 312
Washington, DC 20036
(202) 223-2532
fax: (202) 223-2538
e-mail: info@chn.org
website: www.chn.org

The Coalition on Human Needs is an alliance of national organizations working together to promote public policies that address the needs of low-income and other vulnerable people. The coalition promotes adequate funding for human needs programs, progressive tax policies, and other federal measures to address the needs of low-income and other vulnerable populations. The coalition publishes the *Human Needs Report* newsletter every other Friday when Congress is in session.

Economic Policy Institute (EPI)
1333 H St. NW, Ste. 300, East Tower
Washington, DC 20005-4707
(202) 775-8810
fax: (202) 775-0819
e-mail: epi@epi.org
website: www.epi.org

The EPI is a nonprofit, nonpartisan think tank that seeks to broaden the public debate about strategies to achieve a prosperous and fair economy. The institute conducts original research on economic issues, makes policy recommendations based on its findings, and disseminates its work to the appropriate audiences. Among the books, studies, issue briefs, popular education materials, and various other publications available at the EPI website is the report "Economic Scarring: The Long-Term Impacts of the Recession."

National Alliance to End Homelessness
1518 K St. NW, Ste. 410
Washington, DC 20005
(202) 638-1526
fax: (202) 638-4664
e-mail: naeh@naeh.org
website: www.endhomelessness.org

The National Alliance to End Homelessness is a nonpartisan organization committed to preventing and ending homelessness in the United States. The alliance works collaboratively with the public, private, and nonprofit sectors to build stronger programs and policies that help communities achieve their goal of ending homelessness. The organization provides fact sheets, reports, presentations, briefs, and case studies at its website, including "Rapid Re-housing: Successfully Ending Family Homelessness."

National Coalition for Homeless Veterans (NCHV)
333½ Pennsylvania Ave. SE
Washington, DC 20003-1148
(800) 838-4357
fax: (888) 233-8582
e-mail: info@nchv.org
website: www.nchv.org

The NCHV is a nonprofit organization that works to end homelessness among veterans by shaping public policy, promoting collaboration, and building the capacity of service providers. The coalition operates as a resource and technical assistance center for a national network of agencies that provide emergency and supportive housing, food, health services, job training and placement assistance, legal aid, and case management support for hundreds of thousands of homeless veterans each year. The NCHV publishes information to provide assistance to community and faith-based organizations, government agencies, corporate partners, and the homeless veterans they serve.

National Coalition for the Homeless (NCH)
2201 P St. NW
Washington, DC 20037
(202) 462-4822

fax: (202) 462-4823
e-mail: info@nationalhomeless.org
website: www.nationalhomeless.org

The NCH is a national network of homeless people, activists and advocates, community-based and faith-based service providers, and others committed to ending homelessness. The coalition works to prevent and end homelessness while ensuring that the immediate needs of those experiencing homelessness are met and their civil rights protected. The NCH publishes numerous reports and papers, available at their website, including *Hate Crimes Against the Homeless: Violence Hidden in Plain View.*

National Housing Conference (NHC)
1900 M St. NW, Ste. 200
Washington, DC 20036
(202) 466-2121
fax: (202) 466-2122
website: www.nhc.org

The NHC is a nonprofit organization dedicated to helping ensure safe, decent, and affordable housing for all in America. The conference advocates for policies and legislation that strengthen the nation's housing finance system; prevent foreclosures; improve the coordination of housing, transportation, and energy policy; and assist low- and moderate-income families. The NHC's research affiliate, the Center for Housing Policy, publishes several reports and briefs, including the annual *Housing Landscape.*

National Law Center on Homelessness & Poverty
1411 K St. NW, Ste. 1400
Washington, DC 20005
(202) 638-2535
fax: (202) 628-2737
website: www.nlchp.org

The National Law Center on Homelessness & Poverty works to prevent and end homelessness by serving as the legal arm of the nationwide movement to end homelessness. The center pursues this mission through impact litigation, policy advocacy, and public education. The center publishes a monthly newsletter, *In Just Times*, and periodic reports, including "Beds and Buses: How Affordable Housing Can Help Reduce School Transportation Costs."

National Network for Youth
741 Eighth St. SE
Washington, DC 20003
(202) 783-7949
website: www.nn4youth.org

The National Network for Youth champions the needs of runaway, homeless, and other disconnected youth. The network serves vulnerable youth through advocacy, innovation, and services. The network also publishes several fact sheets and issue briefs, including "Youth Homelessness."

Urban Institute
2100 M St. NW
Washington, DC 20037
(202) 833-7200
website: www.urban.org

The Urban Institute works to foster sound public policy and effective government by gathering data, conducting research, evaluating programs, and educating Americans on social and economic issues. The institute builds knowledge about the nation's social and fiscal challenges through evidence-based research meant to diagnose problems and figure out which policies and programs work best, for whom, and how. The institute publishes policy briefs, commentary, and research reports, including *Housing as a Platform for Formerly Incarcerated Persons*.

Books

Amster, Randall. *Lost in Space: The Criminalization, Globalization, and Urban Ecology of Homelessness*. New York: LFB Scholarly, 2008. Explores the historical and contemporary implications of homelessness, drawing upon academic disciplines and policy concerns ranging from urban geography to legal advocacy.

Edelman, Peter. *So Rich, So Poor: Why It's So Hard to End Poverty in America*. New York: New Press, 2012. Offers an analysis of how the United States can be so wealthy yet have a steadily growing number of unemployed and working poor.

Ellen, Ingrid Gould, and Brendan O'Flaherty, eds. *How to House the Homeless*. New York: Russell Sage Foundation, 2010. Several authors assess the current state of homeless service programs, analyze the most promising policies and programs going forward, and offer a new agenda for future research.

Fitzpatrick, Kevin, and Mark LaGory. *Unhealthy Cities: Poverty, Race, and Place in America*. New York: Routledge, 2011. Brings together research and writing from a variety of disciplines to demonstrate the health costs of being poor in America's cities.

Flowers, R. Barri. *Street Kids: The Lives of Runaway and Thrownaway Teens*. Jefferson, NC: McFarland, 2010. Explores the complex problem of street kids in America and laws and programs designed to combat the commercial sexual exploitation of homeless youth.

Gibson, Kristina E. *Street Kids: Homeless Youth, Outreach, and Policing New York's Streets*. New York: New York University Press, 2011. Argues that public space regulations and policing play a critical role in shaping the experience of youth homelessness and the effectiveness of street outreach.

Gowan, Teresa. *Hobos, Hustlers, and Backsliders: Homeless in San Francisco*. Minneapolis: University of Minnesota Press, 2010. Depicts the lives of homeless men in San Francisco and analyzes the influence of the homelessness industry on the streets, in the shelters, and on public policy.

Karp, Brianna. *The Girl's Guide to Homelessness: A Memoir*. Don Mills, ON: Harlequin, 2011. A young woman recounts her personal experience with homelessness and her experience becoming an activist for the homeless community.

Kozol, Jonathan. *Fire in the Ashes: Twenty-Five Years Among the Poorest Children in America*. New York: Crown, 2012. Tells the story of several young men and women coming of age in the poorest communities of the United States.

Pimpare, Stephen. *A People's History of Poverty in America*. New York: New Press, 2008. Tells real-life stories of those struggling with poverty in America, from the big city to the rural countryside, ranging from the early days of the nation to the present day.

Ryan, Kevin, and Tina Kelley. *Almost Home: Helping Kids Move from Homelessness to Hope*. Hoboken, NJ: Wiley, 2012. Tells the stories of six young homeless people from across the United States and Canada as they confront life alone on the streets.

Schutt, Russell K., with Stephen M. Goldfinger. *Homelessness, Housing, and Mental Illness*. Cambridge, MA: Harvard University Press, 2011. Describes a large-scale study performed to assess how well homeless people with mental illness do when attempts are made to reduce their social isolation and integrate them into the community.

Seider, Scott. *Shelter: Where Harvard Meets the Homeless*. New York: Continuum, 2010. Discusses the operations of the only student-run homeless shelter in the United States, making the case for replication of the model around the country.

Smiley, Tavis, and Cornel West. *The Rich and the Rest of Us: A Poverty Manifesto*. New York: Smiley, 2012. Argues that now is the time to confront the underlying conditions of systemic poverty in America before it is too late.

Wasserman, Jason Adam, and Jeffrey Michael Clair. *At Home on the Street: People, Poverty, and a Hidden Culture of Homelessness*. Boulder, CO: Lynne Rienner, 2010. Argues that programs and policies addressing homeless people too often serve only to alienate them.

Periodicals and Internet Sources

America. "Homeless Soldiers," November 15, 2010.

Anand, Jasleen K. "Supportive Housing as a Solution to Homelessness," *Probate & Property*, July/August 2008.

Anderson, Michelle D. "Special Schools for Homeless Students Bursting at the Seams," *Education Week*, April 2011.

Berg, Nate. "Who's Poor? It Depends on Where You Live, Some Say," *Christian Science Monitor*, August 26, 2008.

Buckley, Cara. "To Test Housing Program, Some Are Denied Aid," *New York Times*, December 8, 2010.

Christian Science Monitor. "Headway with the Homeless," August 28, 2008.

Condon, Sean. "Dollars and Sense: Quantifying the Cost of Homelessness," *This*, January/February 2008.

Diaz, John. "The Issue That Won't Go Away," *San Francisco Chronicle*, June 10, 2012.

Economist. "*Et in Arcadia Ego:* Recession and Homelessness," January 29, 2011.

Ehrenreich, Barbara. "Why Homelessness Is Becoming an Occupy Wall Street Issue," *Mother Jones*, October 24, 2011. www.motherjones.com.

Ertll, Randy Jurado. "Homelessness Must Be Given Top Priority," *Progressive*, April 1, 2009. www.progressive.org.

Esteven, Gregory. "Why Am I Not Surprised? Homelessness, Race, Rita, and Katrina," *Political Affairs*, March 19, 2008.

Falvo, Nick. "Homeless Tide Sure to Rise," *Toronto Star*, July 31, 2010.

Ganeva, Tana. "We're a Country That Lets Kids Go Homeless," AlterNet, July 16, 2012. www.alternet.org.

Garber, Megan. "Wi-Fi Hotspots Made of Homeless People: Not as Horrible as They Seem," *Atlantic*, March 12, 2012. www.theatlantic.com.

Goldstein, Dana. "Rethinking Homelessness," *American Prospect*, September 22, 2008. www.prospect.org.

Heflick, Nathan. "Person or Object? The Case of Homelessness," *Psychology Today*, March 15, 2012.

Hoffman, Nicholas von. "Foreclosed Americans Fight Back," *Nation*, February 23, 2009.

Kalet, Hank. "Evicting the Homeless: Civil Rights for Homeless Communities Wane Across the Country," *In These Times*, July 31, 2012. www.inthesetimes.com.

Kasland, Karen. "Out of Place: For Homeless Teens, Challenges Are Everywhere," *Current Health 2, a Weekly Reader Publication*, March 2010.

Koch, Wendy. "Homelessness in Suburbs, Rural Areas Increases," *USA Today*, July 9, 2009.

Kopp, Emily. "HUD, VA Collaboration Succeeds in Finding Vets Homes," Federal News Radio, January 3, 2012. www.federalnews radio.com.

Lang, James M. "Night Shift: How I Learned to Take Homelessness Personally," *America*, November 21, 2011.

Levenson, Jill S. "Restricting Sex Offender Residences: Policy Implications," *Human Rights*, Spring 2009.

Love, David A. "We Shouldn't Have Homeless Children in America," *Progressive*, September 24, 2009. www.progressive.org.

Mac Donald, Heather. "'Public Interest' Lawyers Say Leave the Homeless to Rot," *Wall Street Journal*, February 14, 2009.

Mangano, Philip. "Ending Homelessness: What Doesn't Work and What Does," *Washington Times*, September 1, 2008.

Markee, Patrick. "The Unfathomable Cuts in Housing Aid," *Nation*, January 2, 2012.

Martin, Courtney. "Homelessness Is Not Just About Housing," *American Prospect*, May 1, 2011. www.prospect.org.

Medved, Diane. "Homeless in Hawaii," Townhall, January 5, 2011. http://townhall.com.

Meyers, Jim. "National Shame: Vets More Likely to Be Homeless," *Newsmax*, February 20, 2011.

Morrison, Patt. "Feed the Homeless, Go to Jail?," *Los Angeles Times*, June 13, 2012.

National Coalition for the Homeless. "Why Are People Homeless?," June 2008. www.nationalhomeless.org.

Noce, Roberto. "Seeking Shelter in Public Parks," *LawNow*, November/December 2010.

Oakley, Deirdre, Erin Ruel, and Lesley Reid. "Public Housing for the Poor: Mend It, Don't End It," *Christian Science Monitor*, January 27, 2010.

Panero, James. "Homelessness, Inc.: The War on the Upper West Side," *New York Post*, July 26, 2012. www.nypost.com.

Parvensky, John. "Homeless Aren't Criminals," *Denver Post*, April 5, 2012.

Philadelphia Inquirer. "Feeding the Homeless Better for Everyone Inside," February 18, 2012.

Ray, Susan L. "A Downward Spiral: Homelessness Among Canadian Forces and Allied Forces Veterans," *Esprit de Corps*, November 2011.

Richards, Sue. "It Starts with a Safe Home and Purpose," *Toronto Globe & Mail*, January 8, 2009.

Scott, Cameron. "Surge of Homeless Vets," *Mother Jones*, November 8, 2007. www.motherjones.com.

Spillman, Brenda C., Jennifer Biess, and Graham MacDonald. "Housing as a Platform for Improving Outcomes for Older Renters," What Works Collaborative, April 2012. www.urban.org.

Sundeen, Mark. "Homeless by Choice: How to Live for Free in America," *Atlantic*, March 7, 2012. www.theatlantic.com.

Terpstra, Ben-Peter. "Obama's America: There's No Place like Homelessness," *American Thinker*, May 31, 2009. www.american thinker.com.

Ulam, Alex. "The Next Big Housing Crisis?," *Nation*, April 4, 2011.

Williams, Leigh Anne. "Anglicans Working to End Homelessness: Need to Debunk Myths and Give Homeless 'Housing First,'" *Anglican Journal*, January 2010.

Websites

Homelessness Resource Center (www.homeless.samhsa.gov). The Homelessness Resource Center is part of the Substance Abuse and Mental Health Services Administration's Recovery Support Strategic Initiative. Its website is an interactive learning community dedicated to disseminating knowledge and best practices to prevent and end homelessness.

US Department of Health and Human Services (www.hhs.gov /homeless). This website contains information on efforts by the department to end homelessness, including information on government grants.

US Interagency Council on Homelessness (www.usich.gov). This website has information about various programs administered by several government agencies to address homelessness.

Index

American Civil Liberties Union (ACLU), 94, 97, 98
American Recovery and Reinvestment Act (2009), 67

Bandow, Doug, 70
Basford, Ron, 14
Bauer, Catherine, 89
Bible, 71
Bloomberg, Michael, 96
Brown, Tim, 60
Bush, George W./Bush administration, 34, 54, 56, 82

Canada
  number of people who experienced homelessness, 15
  size of homeless population in, 12
Canadian Alliance to End Homelessness, 12
Cardin, Benjamin, 110
CBPP (Center on Budget and Policy Priorities), 76
Census Bureau, US, 47
Center for the Study of Hate & Extremism, 110
Center on Budget and Policy Priorities (CBPP), 76

Charity, private
  average contribution of Americans to, 73
  should be used to end homelessness, 70–75
Chen, Michelle, 25
Children/youth, homeless, 109
  benefits of housing vouchers to, 81
  in Cleveland public schools, 31
  crime among, 115–116
  in New York City, 26, 27, 32
  in San Bernardino public schools, 31–32
Christian Science Monitor (newspaper), 52
Chronicle of Philanthropy (journal), *73*
Cleveland (OH)
  Continuum of Care program in, 68
  number of homeless public school students in, 31
Continuum of Care program (Cleveland), 68

Department of Agriculture, US, 47
Department of Housing and Urban Development, US (HUD), 7, 33, 53, 60, 115

economic recession has
  sparked increase in, 25–29
government housing vouchers
  are effective in addressing,
  76–83
government programs can/
  should be used to end,
  63–69
housing-first strategy works to
  decrease, 52–56
is created by deregulation/
  cutback, 11–16
is created by government
  regulation, 17–24
Homeless population(s),
  71–72
in Canada, 12
in New York City shelters,
  27, 32
overall and by
  subpopulations, 2011, *68*
of Sacramento County, 58,
  59
Homeless Prevention and Rapid
  Re-housing Program (HPRP),
  33, 67–68
Homeless system, average costs
  for first-time homeless in, 7
Home ownership, federal
  subsidy programs to
  encourage, 74
Homestead acts, 22
Homicides/homicide rate
  of homeless persons, *114,*
  114–115
national *vs.* for the homeless,
  2009, 115

Hospitalizations, of homeless
  adults, 8
Household(s)
  poor, percentage having
    various amenities, 49
  poverty status for adults, by
    shared household status,
    40
  shared, increased poverty has
    caused increase in, 37–43
  See also Families, homeless
Housing and Community
  Development Act (1974),
  85
Housing Choice Voucher
  Program (Section 8), 77–78
  cuts in, 34
  eligibility for, 78–81
  impacts of, 81–82
  is effective form of assistance,
    76–83
  origins of, 85
  promotes dependency/
    poverty, 84–91
Housing/housing programs
  homelessness is created by
    cutbacks in, 11–16
  substandard, as problem is
    overstated, 44–50
  temporary, chronically
    homeless need more than,
    57–62
  See also Permanent supportive
    housing
Housing vouchers. *See* Housing
  Choice Voucher Program

on homelessness and
employment, 28
on household food security,
47
on organizations doing best job
of feeding the homeless, *72*
on work requirement for
welfare recipients, *86*

Tenant-Based Rental Assistance,
67

Unemployment
among Sacramento homeless,
28

changes in, by state, 35
United Nations, 12

Venkatesh, Sudhir Alladi,
19

Washington Post (newspaper),
27
Williams, Stephen, 99

Yohn, William H., Jr, 96
Youth. *See* Children/youth,
homeless

Zashin, Marcia, 31

Picture Credits

© AP Images, 95

© AP Images/Manuel Baice Ceneta, 46

© AP Images/Bloomington Herald--Times, Jeremy Hogan, 89

© AP Images/Joe Cavaretta, 74

© AP Images/The Charlotte Observer, John D. Simmons, 32

© AP Images/Al Grillo, 65

© AP Images/Rich Pedroncelli, 61

© AP Images/Reed Saxon, 116

© AP Images/Steven Senne, 55

© Kitra Cahana/Getty Images, 39

© Emmanuel Dunand/AFP/Getty Images, 28

© Gale, Cengage, 15, 20, 35, 40, 49, 54, 59, 68, 72, 80, 86, 101, 107, 114

© Toby Jorrin/MCT/Landov, 79

© Peter Kneffel/dpa/Landov, 13

© P.A. Lawrence, LLC/Alamy, 10

© David McNew/Getty Images, 108

© John Moore/Getty Images, 100

© Chip Somodevilla/Getty Images, 51

© Jill Toyoshiba/MCT/Landov, 23

© Tom Williams/Roll Call/Getty Images, 92